SPANISH COMEDY AND HUMOUR

Books LLC®, Reference Series, Memphis, USA, 2011. www.booksllc.net. Copyright: http://creativecommons.org/licenses/by-sa/3.0/deed.en

Table of Contents

Spanish comedians
Andreu Buenafuente 1
Antonia San Juan 2
Berta Collado 2
Berto Romero 3
Carlos Arniches 3
Carlos Latre 4
Charo 4
Chiquito de la Calzada 6
Dani Mateo 7
Eva Hache 7
Florentino Fernández 7
Joaquín Monserrat 8
Joaquín Reyes (actor) 8
Los Payasos de la Tele 9
Luis Piedrahita 10
Miguel Gila 10
Miki Nadal 10
Pablo Motos 11
Paco León 11
Patricia Conde 12
Paz Padilla 12
Pilar Rubio 12
Rodolfo Chikilicuatre 13
Rosa Maria Sardà 14
Secun de la Rosa 14
Señor Wences 15
Vital Aza 17
Yolanda Ramos 17
Ángel Garó 17
Ángel Martín 18

Spanish comedy and humour
El Jueves 18
Generation of '27 19
José Luis Torrente 20

Spanish comedy television series
7 vidas 21
Abdelaziz (TV series) 22
Aquí no hay quien viva 22
Aída 29
El Hormiguero 30
El Intermedio 32
El día después 32
Escenas de Matrimonio 32
Física o Química 34
Goenkale 35
Gominolas 37
La Hora Chanante 37
La que se avecina 38
Las noticias del guiñol 39
Los Serrano 39
Los hombres de Paco 40
Mis adorables vecinos 41
Muchachada Nui 41
Plats bruts 42
Sé lo que hicisteis 42
Vaya Semanita 43
¡Ay, Señor, Señor! 44

Spanish humorists
Enrique Jardiel Poncela 44
Juan José Carbó 44
Pedro Antonio de Alarcón 45

Introduction

Purchase of this book entitles you to a free trial membership in the publisher's book club at www.booksllc.net. (Time limited offer.) Simply enter the barcode number from the back cover onto the membership form. The book club entitles you to select from hundreds of thousands of books at no additional charge. You can also download a digital copy of this and related books to read on the go. Simply enter the title or subject onto the search form to find them.

Each chapter in this book ends with a URL to a hyperlinked online version. Type the URL exactly as it appears. If you change the URL's capitalization it won't work. Use the online version to access related pages, websites, footnotes, tables, color photos, updates. Click the version history tab to see the chapter's contributors. Click the edit link to suggest changes.

A large and diverse editor base collaboratively wrote the book, not a single author. After a long process of discussion and debate, the chapters gradually took on a neutral point of view reached through consensus. Additional editors expanded and contributed to chapters striving to achieve balance and comprehensive coverage. This reduced the regional or cultural bias found in many other books and provided access and breadth on subject matter otherwise little documented.

Andreu Buenafuente

Andreu Buenafuente (Reus, Catalonia, Spain, 24 January 1965) is a Spanish late night show host and founder of the group El Terrat. He has worked in TV3, Antena 3 and La Sexta. He has also worked on the radio and published several books with his monologues.

Career on television

- *Sense Títol* (TV3)
- *Sense Títol 2* (TV3)
- *Sense Títol, Sense Vacances* (TV3)

- *Sense Títol Sense Número* (TV3)
- *La cosa nostra* (TV3)
- *Una altra cosa* (TV3)
- *Buenafuente* (Antena 3)
- *Buenafuente* (La Sexta)

Source (edited): "http://en.wikipedia.org/wiki/Andreu_Buenafuente"

Antonia San Juan

Antonia San Juan (born March 22, 1961), is a Spanish actress, director and screenwriter.

She was born in Las Palmas de Gran Canaria, Spain. At 19 she went to Madrid, where she started working as a professional theatre actress and also as a cabaret act in pubs and bars. She became known thanks to her role as Agrado in *Todo sobre mi madre* by Pedro Almodóvar. A famous Spanish magazine article about her alleged transsexuality caused great controversy. She is well-known in Spain not only because of her film career but also for her humorous monologues on television and theatre. Since 2009 she has been acting in the popular Spanish TV series *La que se avecina*, where her role of Estela Reynolds is one of the most acclaimed roles in the show.

Filmography

- La caja (2006)
- La china (2005)
- Un buen día (2005)
- Un dulce despertar (2005)
- El hambre (2005)
- La maldad de las cosas (2005)
- La nevera (2005)
- Mela y sus hermanas (2004)
- Te llevas la palma (2004)
- 238 (2003)
- Colours (2003)
- Octavia (2002)
- La balsa de piedra (2002)
- Amnèsia (2002)
- Piedras (2002)
- Venganza (2002))
- V.O. (2001)
- El pan de cada día, El (2000)
- Asfalto (2000)
- Ataque verbal (1999)
- Manolito Gafotas (1999)
- Todo sobre mi madre (1999)
- Hongos (1999)
- La primera noche de mi vida (1998)
- El grito en el cielo (1998)
- Perdona bonita, pero Lucas me quería a mí (1997)
- La vida siempre es corta (1994)

Source (edited): "http://en.wikipedia.org/wiki/Antonia_San_Juan"

Berta Collado

Berta Collado (Talavera de la Reina, Toledo, Spain, July 3, 1979) is a Spanish TV presenter and journalist. She grew up in Navalmoral de la Mata, Cáceres, Spain.

Career

She started in journalism when she was 20 in various print and communication offices. She began in television in 2004 in the local network Punto TV belonging to Vocento Group.

In Onda 6 she hosted the second season of the videogame-related program *Do U Play?* and later *Insert Coin* in AXN.

In 2006 she co-hosted in the sports program *Maracaná 06* on Cuatro.

In addition she has worked as a model advertising for several brands such as Deuralde or a video advertising the Spanish Armed Forces.

On November 2005 she joined in the comedy program *Sé lo que hicisteis...* in La Sexta as a reporter of political and sports events. From July 5, 2010 Berta become the host sustitute of the program during Patricia Conde vacations.

She also has appeared in February 2009 the cover of men's magazine FHM and was selected the 22nd sexiest Spanish women by that magazine.

Television

- *Do U Play* (Onda 6).
- *Insert Coin* (AXN and Sony TV)
- *Maracaná 06* (Cuatro).
- *Al salir de clase* (Telecinco).
- *U.V.E* (Cuatro).
- *Como te lo cuento....* (Localia TV).
- *El ojo público* (La Primera de TVE).
- *Esta tarde con esta gente* (Cuatro).
- *Sé lo que hicisteis...* (La Sexta).

Source (edited): "http://en.wikipedia.org/wiki/Berta_Collado"

Berto Romero

Berto Romero

Berto Romero, born November 17, 1974 in Cardona (Catalonia, Spain), is a Spanish humorist.

Biography

He is a member of the theatre company *El Cansancio*, a broadcaster on Ràdio Flaixbac and he has his own segment on Andreu Buenafuente's *late show* on La Sexta (Channel 6). He substituted Buenafuente as host of the show during Summer 2008 (*Buenafuente ha salido un momento*), and resigned for the next season as sub-director of the programme. He got the chance to run his own prime-time weekly show (*El programa de Berto*) on the same channel on 15 March 2009, but the programme was cancelled after just three weeks due to poor results.

Carrer on TV

His first appearances took place in shows of the catalan television TV3, where he hosted a show called "El gran què". Later on he appeared as a monologuist in a show by El Terrat for the private channel 8tv called "Que no surti d'aquí".

Since 2007, he works in the late night show "Buenafuente, first sporadically when the show was still on Antena 3 (where he sang some songs such as "Tunéame Doctor Juan", along with Iván Rodríguez "El lagarto" on guitar) and later on, when Buenafuente got signed up by LaSexta, as a main contributor and scriptwriter. He owned a section called "Bertovisión", where he would analize all media, specially, written articles and where he would also comment the pictures, substituted later on for a news section, along with Andreu Buenafuente. Furthermore, he also participated in "Bertomansión", a project where the viewers would send whatever they did not want or used anymore so he could built a home. Later on, some comedy schetches would take place here. Unlike his radio and theatre appearances, his TV appearances have always been solo.

Taking advantage of his appearances on the media, in April 2008 he edited his first book along with Xavi Tribó, "Cero estrellas" ("Zero Stars"), starring a hypothetical critic, Antonín Fajardo, a character born in a radio collaboration on the show "La taverna del llop" in Ràdio 4.

During the summer of 2008, the channel LaSexta decided that he would be in charge of hosting the show Buenafuente during the holidays of Andreu Buenafuente, giving him that way more responsibility as vicedirector on the show. During this period, the show was broadcasted under the name "Buenafuente ha salido un momento" (Buenafuente will be right back), where he had some sections such as "Rompe el hielo con Berto" (Break the ice with Berto).

March 15, 2009, he made his debut as the host of his own talk show, "El programa de Berto", produced by El Terrat. Nevertheless, the show was suspended after only three shows, since the share was of 3.8%, a number way lower than the average of the channel (6.7% as of March 2009).

April 22, 2009, he participated briefly on the sketch "EL caso del eslabón perdido" in the show Muchachada Nui.

During the season 2009/2010, he started collaborating for the magazine Divendres, broadcasted by TV3, a job he combined with his role in Buenafuente.

October 27, 2009, the TV show Zombis aired on the YouTube channel of El Terrat, starring Berto Romero and Rafel Barceló, scriptwriter for Buenafuente. The show only counts on one season of 9 episodes and since January 28, 2011, it is broadcasted by the channel TNT (Spain).

In New Year's Eve 2009, he hosted, along with Ana Morgade, the New Year's Eve Celebration of LaSexta, entitled "Cómo superar el Fin de Año" (How to get over New Year's Eve). In New Year's Eve 2010, they repeated with "El 2011 con Berto y Ana" (2011 with Berto and Ana.

Source (edited): "http://en.wikipedia.org/wiki/Berto_Romero"

Carlos Arniches

Carlos Arniches (1866–1943) was a Spanish playwright. His work, drawing on the traditions of the género chico, the zarzuela and the grotesque, came to dominate the Spanish comic theatre in the early twentieth century.

Arniches was complimented in a 1935 interview by Federico García Lorca, often a scathing critic of Spanish theatre in the 1920s and 1930s, as 'more of a poet than almost any of those who are writing theatre in verse at the moment'.

Following the consolidation of the Franco regime after the Spanish Civil

Carlos Latre

Carlos Latre, (Castellón de la Plana, January 30, 1979) is a Spanish comedian actor.

He studied until the last year of highschool in the *Institut Martí Franqués* from Tarragona.

He started in several radio stations as a presenter: Ser, 40 Principales or Cadena Dial.

His first TV programme is 1999 TV3 show "Xou com sou" and he became very popular thanks to his impersonations of La Pitonisa Lola, Dinio, Pepe Navarro, Boris Izaguirre, la Duquesa de Alba, Rosa López, Tamara, Jorge Berrocal, Joaquín Sabina, Jesús Quintero, Carmen Vijande, Toni Genil, Leonardo Dantés, José Manuel Parada or la Pantoja de Puerto Rico.

Telecinco gave him a program, *Latrelevisión* and he went later to Cuatro.

He's also a voice actor and has taken part in films like *La increíble pero cierta historia de Caperucita Roja* or *The Jungle Book 2*.

TV

- 1999 TV3, *Xou com sou*
- Telecinco, *Crónicas marcianas*
- 2003 Telecinco, *Latrelevisión*
- 2005-2006 Cuatro, *Maracaná*

Filmography

- *Torrente 3: el protector* (2005)
- *El oro de Moscú* (2003)

Source (edited): "http://en.wikipedia.org/wiki/Carlos_Latre"

Charo

María del Rosario Pilar Martínez Molina Gutiérrez de los Perales Santa Ana Romanguera y de la Hinojosa Rasten (born January 15, 1951), better known as **Charo**, is a Spanish-American actress, comedienne, and flamenco guitarist, best known for her flamboyant stage presence, her provocative outfits, and her trademark phrase ("cuchi-cuchi").

Date of birth

Official documents in Murcia, Spain (where she was born) and the United States indicate she was born in 1941, but Charo has insisted she was born in 1951 and persuaded a United States court to uphold the 1951 birth year as official.

The performer has said in past interviews that her parents allowed her to falsify her age to appear to be older after marrying 66-year-old band leader Xavier Cugat when she was 15. Further complicating the question is the fact that contemporary press reports gave her age at marriage as 21, an April 1966 column on the wedding plans stated she was 20 and Cugat was 60, and columns less than two years before the marriage refer to her as Cugat's "18-year-old protegée" — which, if she was falsifying her age, would have made her actually 13 at the time.

In October 1977 — the same year in which Charo filed for divorce from Cugat and became an American citizen — a United States court upheld the 1951 birth year as official, with the performer providing a sworn statement from her parents in support of her claim. Commenting on the disputes over her age, she has said that the public's disbelief could prove advantageous: "But if people really believe I'm older, that's fine. Don't be surprised if I come out with my own cosmetics, a new energy bar and maybe some vitamins."

Biography

Early life

Charo was born María Hernandez in Murcia, Spain in 1951, Charo's father was a lawyer who reportedly fled to Casablanca during Francisco Franco's dictatorship while her homemaker mother stayed behind in Murcia raising their children. She studied classical and flamenco guitar while residing in Murcia, and can claim Andrés Segovia as her guitar teacher. He once spoke of his pupil in an interview, and remembered giving her career advice. "Stop saying 'cuchi-cuchi' so much, Charo! Be serious!" (Segovia taught general music classes as community service in schools around Murcia.) She took guitar lessons from him and other teachers from the age of nine on. As a result of her training and skill she has been named "Best Flamenco Guitarist" in *Guitar Player Magazine's* readers' poll twice.

When Charo was quite young, she was "discovered" by famous bandleader Xavier Cugat, whom she later wed on August 7, 1966. Cugat was 66 and had already been married four times (Rita Montaner, Carmen Castillo, Lorraine Allen, Abbe Lane) although reports sometimes listed fewer marriages. An April 1966 column by Earl Wilson on the couple's wedding plans announced, *"Sixty-year-old [sic] Xavier Cugat and his 20-year-old Spanish girlfriend and singing star Charo hope to get married in San Cugat, Spain, in a few days – if Cugat can convince church authorities his two divorces should not be counted against him since he wasn't married in church."* The couple was the first to have their nuptials in Caesars Palace in Las Vegas.

In a February 2005 interview with the Los Angeles-based Spanish-language newspaper *La Opinión*, Charo claimed that her marriage to Cugat had been merely a "business contract," a way for him to legally bring her over to the United States, where he was based.

She moved to West 257th Street in the New York City borough of The Bronx with her mother and aunt, and was regularly featured in shows with Cugat's orchestra in New York and Las Vegas, as well as in overseas engagements in Latin America and Europe. She claims he was confident in her eventual success from early on, and that she gave him a Rolls-Royce as a parting gift once she came of legal age.

Career

Charo's first US TV appearance was on *The Today Show* in the mid-1960s. She later appeared on *Laugh-In* in 1968. She would appear on short chatfests of a few minutes near the end of the show with Dan Rowan and Dick Martin. Her almost complete lack of fluency in the English language was played as a comic focus, and she would have the two hosts laughing at her mangled English. This is also the time that the "cuchi cuchi' line passed into the public arena.

The 1970s

She was headlining Vegas shows by 1971, and reportedly being paid as much as Frank Sinatra, Ray Charles or Dean Martin. In 1977, she became a naturalized citizen of the United States; that same year, she filed for divorce from Cugat, a petition that was granted April 14, 1978 On August 11, 1978, she married her second husband, Kjell Rasten, a producer, in South Lake Tahoe, California, in a civil ceremony attended by 30 guests. Rasten soon became his wife's manager, and the couple has one child, a son, Shel Rasten (born 1982), who is the drummer for the heavy metal band Treazen.

Throughout the 1970s, she was a highly visible personality, appearing 8 times on *The Love Boat*, as well as on variety and talk shows such as *Donny & Marie, Tony Orlando and Dawn, The Captain and Tennille, The John Davidson Show, The Mike Douglas Show*, which she guest-hosted at least once, and even the infamously short-lived *Brady Bunch* variety spinoff.

In 1975, *Dallas Morning News* critic Harry Bowman wrote that the ABC network had "penciled in ... a half-hour comedy starring the uninhibited wife of Xavier Cugat" and commented, "This is probably the worst idea of the season." By October of that year, the performer was promoting a special slated for November, but the special did not actually appear until May, 1976. A TV listing for August 24, 1976, shows what appears to be an unsold pilot airing on ABC at 8:30 pm CST: "*Charo and the Sergeant* - Situation comedy starring Charo Cugat. Charo's first U.S. job is to be a dancer at an off-limits night club, and her conservative Marine Corps husband finds out. The few episodes that were taped ended up being broadcast on the American Armed Forces Network overseas. "

By the late 1970s, Charo was being mentioned as an example of how overexposure could damage a celebrity; one such article quoted Steve Levitt's "Q score" research to show the performer's popularity declined slightly even as her familiarity increased:

> Before she gained national fame on talk shows in 1975, bosomy Latin starlet Charo was 'recognized' by 57 per cent of Levitt's national television sample - and had a 'popularity quotient' of 9 per cent. Today, known by 80 per cent, a figure as high as Clint Eastwood's 80 per cent, Charo's popularity is 8 per cent. 'If she was known by 100 per cent of the world, chances are her popularity might go down to 7 or 6 per cent', Levitt says coolly. That paradox makes some performers think twice when invitations to talk shows come in.

—*"The TV Talk Shows", Washington Post, July 14, 1977 (Style section, page B1)*

Post-1970s

For much of the late 1980s and 1990s Charo had limited visibility as she moved to Hawaii, and opened and performed at her own dinner theater while she and Rasten raised their son. Because of the large number of Japanese immigrants to the island state, Charo learned to speak Japanese. In the 2000s, she returned to television in commercials for Sprint wireless phone service and GEICO insurance, as well as guest appearances on Hollywood Squares, a season-three stint on the celebreality series *The Surreal Life*, as guest appearances on the Fox Network's *That '70s Show* and appearances in VH1's *I Love the '70s* retrospectives. Most recently, on May 11, 2008. she made a guest appearance on the Latin-themed VH1 reality show *Viva Hollywood*.

Most recently

She now has a regular touring show in addition to appearances in Branson, Missouri, and Las Vegas (which at one time were choreographed by Comedy Central actor/dancer Jade Esteban Estrada). Charo appeared as the Celebrity Showtime entertainer aboard Royal Caribbean Explorer of the Seas on its January 4 & January 13, 2008 sailings, and on the Adventure of the Seas on its August 10, 2008 sailing. She was a Celebrity Grand Marshal of the San Francisco LGBT Pride Parade on Sunday, June 29, 2008. She was accompanied by hordes of Charo lookalikes on a pink float. On May 23, 2008, she was a guest on *GSN Live*.

She returned to the dance music scene in June 2008 with the single "España Cañi". The single was released through Universal Wave Records. She performed Rihanna's song "Don't Stop the Music" at the 2009 Muscular Dystrophy Association Jerry Lewis Labor Day Telethon.

Charo appeared as the Celebrity Showtime entertainer aboard Royal Caribbean Liberty of the Seas cruise ship on Christmas Eve, 2009. She also appeared on the Royal Caribbean ship Adventure of the Seas on Thursday, February 25, 2010. She continues to entertain guests on Royal Caribbean Serenade of the Seas in May 2010. In April 2010, she made a guest appearance on *Dancing with the Stars*. In 2010, she made a guest appearance on the Disney television show, *The Suite Life on Deck*. Charo made an appearance on "Watch What Happens Live!" on February 22, 2011 where she promoted a new song, "Sexy! Sexy!".

Discography

Albums

- *Cuchi-Cuchi* (1977) (with the Salsoul Orchestra)
- *Olé Olé* (1978) (with the Salsoul Orchestra)
- *Bailando con Charo* (*Dancing with Charo*, 1981) (with the Salsoul Orchestra)
- *Guitar Passion* (1994)
- *Blame It on the Macarena* (1996)
- *Gusto* (*Pleasure*, 1997)
- *Charo and Guitar* (2005)

Singles

- 1976: "La Salsa"
- 1977: "Dance A Little Bit Closer" (US Dance #18)
- 1978: "Mamacita, ¿dónde está Santa Claus? (Mommy, Where's Santa Claus?)"
- 1978: "Olé Olé" (US Dance #36)
- 1979: "Stay With Me" (US Dance #55)
- 1979: "Hot Love"
- 1981: "La Mojada (Wet Back)"
- 2003: "Prisionera De Tu Amor" (with Seductive Souls)
- 2008: "España Cañi" (US Dance #14)
- 2011: "Sexy Sexy" (US Dance #47)

Filmography

- *Don Juan Tenorio* (1952) (unconfirmed)
- *Tiger by the Tail* (1969)
- *Elvis: That's the Way It Is* (1970) (documentary)
- *The Concorde ... Airport '79* (1979)
- *Moon Over Parador* (1988)
- *Thumbelina* (1994) (voice)

Television work

- *The Hollywood Squares* (semi-regular panelist from 1972–1978)
- *The Charo Show* (1976) (unsold pilot for variety series)
- *Chico and the Man* (cast member from 1977–1978)
- *The Love Boat* (guest starred in 8 episodes, 1977–1984)
- *Fantasy Island* (guest starred in 4 episodes, 1981–1984)
- *The Facts of Life* (guest appearance in 1985)
- *Marblehead Manor* (Feb 18, 1988)
- *Pee-wee's Playhouse Christmas Special* (guest star 1988)
- *Olivia Mayo is Life* (special appearance November 20, 1992)
- *Mickey Mouse Works* (special guest voiceover)
- *That '70s Show* (special guest star: "Red Sees Red" 2000)
- *Space Ghost Coast to Coast* (unaired interview, but was quickly glimpsed on Episode 60: "Lawsuit" 1998)
- *The Brak Show* (special guest star 2001)
- *The Surreal Life* (cast member in 2004)
- *So NoTORious* (episode 5, season 1 in 2006)
- *I Love the '70s: Volume 2* (appearances in 2006)
- *Chappelle's Show* (appearance in 2006)
- *Las Vegas*
- *Sprint Cellular Phones* featuring the catch phrase "I thought you said bring home Charo"
- *Geico Auto Insurance Commercial* (Acts out the Geico customer's experience 2007)
- *Viva Hollywood!* New reality show on VH1 May 11, 2008)
- *Tonight Show with Jay Leno* (special appearance April 17, 2008)
- *Chelsea Lately* (special appearance July 24, 2008)
- *Tonight Show with Jay Leno* (special appearance Dec 18, 2008)
- *RuPaul's Drag Race* (guest performer Mar 9, 2009)
- *The Suite Life on Deck* (special appearance as Esteban's mother in 2010)
- *Good Luck Charlie* (special appearance as girl crushing on Bob Duncan)

Source (edited): "http://en.wikipedia.org/wiki/Charo"

Chiquito de la Calzada

Gregorio Esteban Sánchez Fernández (born 24 October 1932 in Málaga), known as **Chiquito de la Calzada**, is a Spanish flamenco singer and actor, although he is more famous as a stand-up comedian. Chiquito de la Calzada became very popular in Spanish TV shows (especially "Genio y Figura") during the mid-nineties due to his unique style, strongly based on a surreal approach to jokes and language. Some of his characteristic words and expressions quickly became memes and are now part of Spanish slang. His moves and jargon were so influential to other Spanish comedians, that some TV characters such as Crispín Klander, Lucas Grijander and Nuñito de la Calzada were entirely built around his own repertoire. There is a mod for the video game *Doom* featuring his voice.

Filmography

- La venganza de Ira Vamp, 2010
- Spanish Movie, 2009
- Franky Banderas, 2003
- El Oro de Moscú, 2002
- Papá Piquillo, 1998
- Brácula (Condemor II), 1997
- Aquí Llega Condemor (El Pecador de la Pradera), 1996

Source (edited): "http://en.wikipedia.org/wiki/Chiquito_de_la_Calzada"

Dani Mateo

Daniel Mateo Patau (Barcelona, Spain, on June 1, 1979) is a comedian, actor and Spanish presenter of radio and television who nowadays is employed at the program of La Sexta: Sé lo que hicisteis...

Licensed in Journalism for the Autonomous University of Barcelona, he initiated his path in the local radio. Later there passed for several professional issuers of Cataluña como: Catalunya Cultura, Onda Cero, Radio Gràcia, Onda Catalana, RAC 1 y Flaix FM.

Is from his friendship with Martin Piñol, he knows in the radio, when he gets squarely into the world of the monologues and Paramount Comedy begins to form a part of the humorists' staff of the television channel.

He has been employed at the Television of Cataluña (TV3), has been a collaborator in different radio stations and, from April, 2004 he presented the program In Noche Sin Tregua (NST) in Paramount Comedy, program that also he would emit during a time Localia TV every Thursday night. He collaborated in the program Phenomena and in the wireless program Fenómenos, of The 40 Principales. Nowadays, he collaborates as columnist in the magazine DT and Jorge Magariño's role interprets in the television series of Antenna 3 La Familia Mata. This personage in a beginning was secondary, but Daniel Guzman's abandon and other factors did that his role was climbing more positions up to managing to appear in the initial head-board.

On November 5, 2007 he joined to the program of La Sexta, Sé Lo Que Hicisteis ... as commentator of today's news and sports. In the program, to report of his section, he takes part also in sketches of the program close to the rest of the distribution, realizing interpretations of prominent figures as Dani Güiza, Jordi (a fan of the Barça), Flipy or El Esmirriao (affectionate nickname on the part of the program to Isaac, Falete's Exboyfriend), and shares a small section dedicated to the current importance of the qualified television what is happening? (Previously what is happening in Telecinco?) with Ángel Martin, his companion of work and great friend with the one that shared flat in Barcelona. Working in Sé Lo Que Hicisteis, interpret monologues in places of the whole Spain.

Source (edited): "http://en.wikipedia.org/wiki/Dani_Mateo"

Eva Hache

Eva Hache (born in Segovia, Castilla and León on 7 August 1972) is a Spanish comedy actress and television show hostess, better known for her late night show *Noche Hache*. Her real name is Eva Hernández.

Biography

After majoring in English, Hache began her career as an actress doing theatre plays. She performed in several classical plays with director Juan Antonio Quintana's company at the *Aula de Teatro* of the *Universidad de Valladolid*. After four years of doing this, she decided to take some free time to travel around the world, and on her return on 2000 played in a self-produced cabaret piece, *Todo por la Talanga, el Chou*, in which the audience played an active role.

She managed to do monologues in several programs for the Paramount Comedy channel until, in 2003, she won the 4th Monologue Contest from the Comedy Club (*Club de la Comedia*). After that, she was hired by producer-company Globomedia, which decided she should accompany Manel Fuentes, conductor of the late night show, *Fuentes y cia*, where she would play a comic reporter. She achieved popularity in the show, which enabled her to participate in other shows, such as *Splunge* (a comic sketches show), and make punctual appearances as an actress in television series, like the popular *7 Vidas* and *Casi Perfectos*.

As a theatre actress, she had main roles in *5mujeres.com* (2003–2004) and *Hombres, mujeres y punto* (2004–2005). Eva has performed in films too, most notably in *Locos por el sexo*, directed by Javier Rebollo. She has also done radio performances, in Cadena Ser's *La ventana del verano*, conducted with Gemma Nierga.

After that, and still under contract with Globomedia, Hache became the hostess of the late night show *Noche Hache*, from Cuatro TV. This show has signified her first job as main hostess of a program, and a success for Cuatro.

She won the 2005 Academy of Television (ATV) Prize, in Best Communicator of Entertaining Programs category. That same year she was also nominated for the TP de Oro (considered to be the most prestigious Spanish award for television) for Best Entertainment Program Hostess.

Source (edited): "http://en.wikipedia.org/wiki/Eva_Hache"

Florentino Fernández

Florentino Fernández Román, *Flo*, (Sacedón, Guadalajara, November 9, 1972) is a Spanish actor, comedian, conductor and showman.

He worked as a security guard before taking part in TV shows like *Esta noche cruzamos el Mississippi* or La Sonrisa del Pelícano with Pepe Navarro, where he impersonated Chiquito de la Calzada and created new characters such as Lucas Grijánder or Krispín Klander.

He went on working in TV programs like "El informal" as a conductor; "Siete Vidas", as an actor; or "El Club de la Comedia", as a monologist.

He dubbed Mike Myers in Austin Powers: The Spy Who Shagged Me and Austin Powers in Goldmember and he performed in the theatre show "5hombres.com" as a monologist.

In movies, he made his first appearances in films like "El oro de Moscú" or "Una de zombis", he made some cameos in films like *Torrente 2* and *Torrente 3* and he had a leading role with Santiago Segura, in *Isi/Disi, Amor a lo Bestia*.

Movies

- 2006
  - *Isi/Disi, Alto Voltaje* by Miguel Ángel Lamata as *Disi*
- 2005
  - *Robots* by Chris Wedge and Carlos Saldanha as *Manivela* (voice).
  - *Torrente 3* by Santiago Segura as *Hombre del lavabo*.
  - *Valiant* by Gary Chapman as *Bugsy* (voz).
- 2004
  - *Isi/Disi* by Chema de la Peña as *Disi*.
- 2003
  - *Una de zombis* by Miguel Ángel Lamata as *Zombi Incompetente*.
  - *El oro de Moscú* by Jesús Bonilla.

Teatre

- 5hombres.com 2003

TV

Actor

- 7 vidas - Telecinco as *Félix Gimeno Huete*
- La Sonrisa del Pelícano 1997 - Antena 3 as *Lucar Grijander* y *Kripín Klander*
- Esta noche cruzamos el Mississippi 1995 - Telecinco *idem*
- Espejo secreto 1997 - TVE

Conductor

- Tonterías las justas 2010 - Cuatro
- El club de Flo 2006 - La Sexta
- Planeta finito 2006 - La Sexta
- Splunge 2005 TVE
- UHF 2003 - Antena 3
- El Show de Flo 2002 - TVE
- El Club de la Comedia 1999 - Canal Plus
- El Informal 1999 - Telecinco

Source (edited): "http://en.wikipedia.org/wiki/Florentino_Fern%C3%A1ndez"

Joaquín Monserrat

Joaquín Monserrat, known as **Pacheco** (April 5, 1921 - November 5, 1996) was a Spanish comedian and host of children programs. Since 1960, he established in Puerto Rico where he became one of the most known and loved hosts of children programs.

Biography

Joaquín Monserrat was born April 5, 1921 in Barcelona. In 1951, he moved to Havana, Cuba, where he worked as a comedian for nine years in CMQ Television. In 1960, he moved to Puerto Rico and was hired as a scriptwriter and comedian in the program *Pacheco, Detective Privado*.

In 1962, he was hired by WAPA-TV, creating the children program *Cine Recreo*. In the program, Monserrat (now known simply as Pacheco) gave the children advice, interviews, and showed cartoons. One of the most emblematic traits of the show was the portrayal of drawings done by children that watched the show and sent them to Pacheco. The show stayed as one of the children favorite since the 60s until the 90s.

Pacheco then created the game show *Contra el Reloj*. For 13 years, he hosted the Jerry Lewis MDA Telethon in the island and occupied the position of Honorary Vicepresident.

In 1987, he organized the first familiar "bicicletada" (bike marathon) with the participation of 15,000 people. The second "bicicletada" had the participation of 30,000 from all ages, being registered in the Guinness Book of World Records by its attendance.

Pacheco died November 5, 1996.
Source (edited): "http://en.wikipedia.org/wiki/Joaqu%C3%ADn_Monserrat"

Joaquín Reyes (actor)

Joaquín Reyes Cano (Albacete, August 16, 1974) is a Spanish actor, draftsman and comedian. He currently manages the humorist sitcom *Museo Coconut* at NEOX, a TDT channel of Antena 3, playing the role of Onofre. He previously worked on the TVE program *Muchachada Nui*, La Hora Chanante) in La 2, *Fibrilando* and *Camera Café* (Telecinco); and collaborates for the radio program *No Somos Nadie* (M80).

Reyes studied Fine Arts at the University of Castile-La Mancha and he has worked as an illustrator for publications like "El barco de vapor" or *Zumo de lluvia*, by Teresa Broseta.

Joaquín Reyes as Tim Burton together with Ernesto Sevilla as Bitelchús (Beetlejuice).

In 2002, he joined Ernesto Sevilla, Pablo Chiapella and Raúl Cimas, the so-called "Trío de Albacete" ("Albacete's Trio", they were all from that province) for the Paramount Comedy program *La Hora Chanante*.

Joaquín Reyes, 2008

Filmography
- *La Crisis Carnívora*, 2006
- *La Gran Revelación*, 2004
- *Spanish Movie*, 2009

Television
- *Muchachada Nui* (2007-), La 2
- *Camera Café* (2005-), Richard, Telecinco
- *La Hora Chanante* (2002–2006), Paramount Comedy
- *A Pelo* (2006–2007), La Sexta
- *Nuevos Cómicos* (2001), Paramount Comedy
- *¡Salvemos Eurovisión!* (2008), La 1
- *Planeta Finito* en Escocia (2007), La Sexta
- *Lo + Plus* (2004–2005), Roberto Picazo, Canal+
- *Smonka!* (2005), Onofre, Paramount Comedy
- *Noche sin tregua* (2004–2006), Roberto Picazo, Paramount Comedy
- *Miradas 2* (2007), TVE
- *Cámara Abierta 2.0* (2007), TVE
- *Informe Semanal* (2007), TVE
- *Silenci?* (2006), TV3

Radio
- *No somos nadie*, M80 Radio

Drawings
- Colección **El barco de vapor**
  - El club de los coleccionistas de noticias
- **Zumo de lluvia** de Teresa Broseta
- Colección *Grupo SM*
  - *Latín. Diccionario didáctico*
  - *Valencià 3º E.P. Nou Projecte Terra.*
- Editorial *Cruïlla*
  - Ortografía castellana elemental
- El País
  - Summer supplements 2007–2008.

Source (edited): "http://en.wikipedia.org/wiki/Joaqu%C3%ADn_Reyes_(actor)"

Los Payasos de la Tele

Los Payasos de la Tele (English: *The TV Clowns*) is the name by which a trio of popular Spanish clowns are known, initially formed by **Gaby** (Gabriel Aragón), **Fofó** (Alfonso Aragón) and **Miliki** (Emilio Aragón), and succeeded by **Fofito** (Alfonso Aragón Jr.), **Milikito** (Emilio Aragón Jr.) and **Rody** (Rody Aragón). They were well-known on Spanish language television in Latin America throughout much of the twentieth century before returning to Spain and attaining further success.

History

Heirs of a long family tradition of circus performance, which stretches back to the nineteenth century, they were sons of Emilio Aragón the elder and nephews of José María and Teodoro Aragón - Emig, Pompoff y Teddy. Other members of the family with circus connections included their cousins Nabucodonosorcito and Zampabollos.

Gaby, Fofó y Miliki began their activities in Spain in 1939 at the Circo Price. In 1946, the three brothers emigrated across the Atlantic, where they remained for more than a quarter of a century. They first set up shop in Cuba, where they made their first incursions into the world of television in 1949. In the following years, the diffusion of their shows in other countries in Latin America made them familiar faces in Mexico, Venezuela, Puerto Rico, and the United States.

In 1970 they arrived in Argentina, and achieved great success through their program *El zapato rojo* (The Red Shoe), which they then renamed *El show de Gaby, Fofó y Miliki*. Soon a new member of the family, *Fofito* (the son of Fofó), made appearances.

Two years later, in 1972, they returned to Spain, contracting with Televisión Española to front a new program called *El Gran Circo de TVE*. It was a great success, remaining on air until 1981, and became an enormous cultural phenomenon in Spain in the 1970s. The group was awarded a TP de Oro, a prestigious Spanish television award, for "most popular personality" in 1974.

After the death of Fofó in 1976, the son of Miliki, Emilio Aragón Jr., joined the group under the name *Milikito*. He is a mute clown, in the tradition of Harpo Marx, and communicates with a cow bell. Much later, after the show ended in 1981, *Rody*, the youngest son of Fofó, joined the group in the persona of a black Cuban.

Finally, the program (which in its final form was called *El loco mundo de los payasos*, or "The Crazy World of the Clowns"), was retired from Spanish television in 1983. After several circus tours during the following two years, under the title *El fabuloso mundo del circo* (The Fabulous World of the Circus), the group (which by this time Miliki had already left) dissolved definitively.

Songs
- Hola, Don Pepito (music and lyrics written by the famous Puerto Rican actor/comedian Ramón Rivero (Diplo))
- *La gallina turuleca* (Spanish version of ¨A galinha magricela¨ from the Brazilian songwriter Edgard Poças)
- *Susanita*
- *Mi barba tiene tres pelos*
- *Un barquito de cáscara de nuez*
- *El auto feo* (original from Pipo Pescador)
- *El sombrero de Fofó*
- *Cómo me pica la nariz*
- *Qué nos da el cerdito*
- *Chinita tú*
- *Una sonrisa y una flor*
- *En la autocaravana*
- *Feliz en tu día*
- *Dale Ramón*
- *Había una vez un circo*

Films
- *Los Padrinos*
- *Había una vez un circo*

Source (edited): "http://en.wikipedia.org/wiki/Los_Payasos_de_la_Tele"

Luis Piedrahita

Luis Piedrahita at 43rd KVIFF

Luis Piedrahita Cuesta (born 1977 in Coruña, Spain) is a Spanish stand-up comedian, magician, script writer, broadcaster and author. He is known as "El Rey de las Cosas Pequeñas" ("The King of Small Things"), due to his monologues in which he critiques the lack of regard of everyday things such as toilet lids, carnivorous plants, etc.

He became widely known as scriptwriter in three seasons of the Spanish TV program *El Club de la Comedia* (*The Comedy Club*). In addition to working on the series *Partners in Crime* for Columbia Tri Star Pictures in Los Angeles, US, he occasionally collaborates in the Spanish TV program El Hormiguero. He has published two books: *Un cacahuete flotando en una piscina* ("A peanut floating in a swimming pool", 2005) and *¿Cada cuánto hay que echar a lavar un pijama?* ("How often should you wash your pyjamas?", 2006)

In 1999 he won the Spanish *Premio Nacional de Magia* (National Magic Award).

He co-directed and co-wrote the 2007 thriller *La habitación de Fermat*, later released internationally as *Fermat's Room*.

He has been collaborating with his writing partner Roberto Sopeña for more than 12 years, since they went together to the university. They wrote a script for an animation Spanish studio Ilion Animation Studios and their next project will be *Golpe de efecto*, a heist movie "with no guns" that they plan to shoot in late 2009 or early 2010.

Source (edited): "http://en.wikipedia.org/wiki/Luis_Piedrahita"

Miguel Gila

Miguel Gila (12 March 1919 – 13 July 2001) was a Spanish comedian actor. He appeared in 27 films and television shows between 1954 and 1993. He starred in the film *¡Viva lo imposible!*, which was entered into the 8th Berlin International Film Festival. He spent some time incarcerated in the Carabanchel Prison because of having joined to the defeated side in the Spanish Civil War. He became famous in Spain and Latin America with his comic monologues.

Selected filmography
- *Adventures of the Barber of Seville* (1954)
- *Uncle Hyacynth* (1956)
- *¡Viva lo imposible!* (1958)

Source (edited): "http://en.wikipedia.org/wiki/Miguel_Gila"

Miki Nadal

Miguel Nadal Furrier (born on September 29, 1967 in Zaragoza, Spain), better known as Miki Nadal, is a Spanish comedian and actor known for his work on television and in the theatre. He studied law but abandoned his studies for the stage. He started his television career in *La sonrisa del pelícano* (literally "The smile of the pelican") in 1997.

He joined the team of *El Informal]* in 1999, in the second season of the program. In the beginning he doubled sequences with Florentino Fernandez, but little by little it he was became a leading protagonist on the program which lasted until April 2002. He has worked in others programs such as *El show de Flo* and *El club de la comedia*.

In 2006, Miki joined La Sexta, where he began with a segment in the special programs that the chain dedicated to the Fifa World Cup 2006. He has appeared as a guest in series such as *Casi perfectos* and *7 vidas* with Florentino Fernandez. In 2010 he joined *Sé lo que hicisteis...* on La Sexta, presenting Internet videos and comdey sketches.

Source (edited): "http://en.wikipedia.org/wiki/Miki_Nadal"

Pablo Motos

Pablo Motos (born August 31, 1965, Requena, Valencia, Spain) is the host of *El Hormiguero*, a popular Spanish television show.

Source (edited): "http://en.wikipedia.org/wiki/Pablo_Motos"

Pablo Motos in *El Hormiguero*.

Paco León

Paco León in 2008.

Paco León and Carmen Machi.

Paco León (born October 4, 1974) is a Spanish comic actor born in Seville. His first television experiences were playing in the childlike comedy "Mariquilla Ríe Perlas" and "Castillos en el Aire" on Canal Sur. He was a host of the variety TV show "Cita a Ciegas" and of the TV game show "Triunfa en Casa." He also played the role of Maria in the comedy "Moncloa, ¿Dígame?" on Telecinco. But his real trampoline to fame was the Antena 3 comedy sketch show Homo Zapping, in which he immediately stood out from among the cast. He has returned to Telecinco with the role of Luisma in Aída.

Filmography

Television

- *Castillos en el aire* (1999) on Canal Sur
- *Jet Lag* (2000)
- *Moncloa, digame* on Telecinco, FDF
- *Homo Zapping* on Antena 3 TV (2003–2005)
- *Siete vidas* on Telecinco (2004, 2005)
- *Aída* on Telecinco (2005-currently)
- *Planeta Finito* on La Sexta (2007)
- *Ácaros* on Cuatro (2007)

Films

- *Amar y Morir en Sevilla, Don Juan Tenorio* (2001) by Victor Barrera
- *Asalto informatico* (2002)
- *La vida mancha* (2003)
- *Recambios* (2004)
- *La Dama Boba* (2006)
- *Los mánagers* (2006)
- *Queens (Reinas)* (2006)

Short films

- La grieta by Enrique López de Haro
- Días rojos (2004)
- Con lengua (2006)

- Espagueti western (2007) (Voice)

Source (edited): "http://en.wikipedia. org/wiki/Paco_Le%C3%B3n"

Patricia Conde

Patricia Conde Galindo (Valladolid, 5 October 1979) is a Spanish actress, comedian, TV presenter and model.

She is the second of three siblings (Nacho and Rubén Conde) and she started to work as a model when she was 14 years old. In 1999 she took part in Miss Spain as Miss Palencia and soon after, she started to work in television. He has worked in several TV shows. Nowadays she presents Se lo qué hicisteis.

TV

- *El informal*, (Telecinco) 2000-2002
- *El club de la comedia*, Canal Plus
- *Lady Kaña*, Telemadrid, 2004
- *Un domingo cualquiera*, TVE, 2004 with Ramón García

Sé lo que hicisteis..., Conde with Ángel Martín

- *Nuestra mejor canción*, TVE, 2004 with Concha García Campoy
- *Splunge*, TVE, 2005
- *7 días desnudo*, Cuatro, 2005–2006
- *Sé lo que hicisteis...*, la Sexta, since march 2006, with Ángel Martín, before called *Sé lo que hicisteis la última semana*.

Theatre

- *5 mujeres.com*
- *Noche de cómicos*
- *Los 39 escalones* (adaptation of *The 39 Steps* by Alfred Hitchcock)

Filmography

- *La Kedada*
- *Tweester Links*

Source (edited): "http://en.wikipedia. org/wiki/Patricia_Conde"

Paz Padilla

Paz Padilla (Seville, 1969) is a Spanish comedian and actress.

After working in Cadiz hospital, she first appeared in an Antena 3 TV programme in 1994. She made lots of collaborations in several programme of this channel, TVE and the channels of the Spanish autonomous communities.

Between 1997 and 1999, she worked for the famous TV programme *Crónicas Marcianas*. After that, she has worked for several TV programmes as a conductor or as an actress in TV series like *Aladina* or *Mis adorables vecinos*. In November of 2009 she hosted "Sálvame", a program with a large audience in Telecinco (fifth channel).

She has worked for radio broadcastings in COPE, in theatre thanks to El Terrat, and in movies like 1999 *Raluy, una noche en el circo* or *Marujas asesinas* in 2001.

Source (edited): "http://en.wikipedia. org/wiki/Paz_Padilla"

Pilar Rubio

Pilar Rubio Fernández (Torrejón de Ardoz, Community of Madrid, Spain March 17, 1978) is a Spanish reporter and TV presenter. She became famous for covering events for the program *Sé lo que hicisteis...* for the television network La Sexta. She is also the girlfriend of the singer of the musical group Hamlet.

Trajectory

She began to study Economics, although she did not finish the degree. She has modelled in several men's magazines, and appeared in the movies *Isi & Disi, alto voltaje* and *Carlitos y el campo de los sueños*, also appearing in two shorts: *Merry Christmas* of Fran Casanova and *Cuestión de química* of Juan Moya, acting along with Cristina Peña and Arturo Valls among others. In television she has appeared in commercials Amstel, Canal+, Hyundai and in programs like *Lo que necesitas es amor*, *The Price Is Right*, *La azotea de Wyoming* and in *Six pack*, broadcast by the network Cuatro.

Her definitive success with the public was her appearance in the comedy program *Sé lo que hicisteis...* of La Sexta, in which she looked at diverse news articles. In the summer of 2007 in addition she appeared in humorous homemade videotapes program called *La ventana indiscreta*.

She won the award of best television reporter with Premio Joven 2007. In 2008 and 2009 she was selected as the sexiest women by the Spanish edition of the FHM magazine.

From July 14 to August 29, 2008 and in July 2009 she presented the program *Sé lo que hicisteis...* replacing Patricia Conde, who was on vacation.

She is currently working for the television network Telecinco.

Televisión

Pilar Rubio covering the Spanish general election, 2008.

- *Lo que necesitas es amor*, Antena 3.
- *The Right Price*, TVE.
- *Esto es vida*, TVE.
- *La azotea de Wyoming*, TVE.
- *Six pack*, Cuatro.
- *Sé lo que hicisteis la última semana*, La Sexta.
- *Sé lo que hicisteis...* (reporter), La Sexta.
- *La ventana indiscreta* (presenter), La Sexta.
- *Adivina quién es quién* (presenter), Canal Sur 2.
- *¡Más que baile!* (presenter), Telecinco.
- *Operación Triunfo* (presenter), Telecinco.

Filmography

- *Merry Christmas* (Short subject).
- *Cuestión de química* (Short subject).
- *Isi & Disi, alto voltaje* (feature film).
- *Carlitos y el campo de los sueños* (feature film).
- Video clip of Hamlet - Limítate
- Video clip de Hombres G - No te escaparás.
- Video clip of David Bustamante - Por Ella.

Source (edited): "http://en.wikipedia.org/wiki/Pilar_Rubio"

Rodolfo Chikilicuatre

Rodolfo Chikilicuatre (born 1972 in Buenos Aires, Argentina); is a Spanish comedic character played by **David Fernández Ortiz** (24 June 1970 in Igualada, Barcelona, Spain) and first introduced in the Spanish late night show *Buenafuente* as an improvisational act. Rodolfo was interviewed as the inventor of the vibrator-guitar. The character rose to fame after he was later presented by the show's host, Andreu Buenafuente, with a song called "**Baila el Chiki-chiki**" (Dance the Chiki-chiki), a parody of reggaeton music filled with jokes and political references, and the show's host decided to enter the song into the Spanish selection process for the Eurovision Song Contest 2008, Rodolfo landed Spains best placement since Eurovision Song Contest 2004.

Eurovision Song Contest 2008 and "Baila el Chiki-chiki"

For the Eurovision Song Contest 2008, the Spanish broadcaster RTVE decided to make the song selection process more democratic, so, in an agreement with MySpace, a webpage was created where the general public could vote for any of the artists who were interested in participating, possibly discovering new talents. Any aspiring singer could upload a video to enter the contest. The top 5 voted videos, along with 5 more entries selected by a jury, went to a televised final where the Spanish Eurovision Song Contest 2008 entry would be chosen.

David Fernández as himself

More than 530 songs were submitted, the comedic act of Rodolfo Chikilicuatre and his "Baila el Chiki-chiki" song among them. The song was heavily promoted by the late show "Buenafuente" and the TV Station LaSexta where the show is broadcasted, and ended up being selected by a landslide, earning 56.28% of the votes, well ahead of the second place, which earned only 14.6%. The winner was chosen through text messaging.

This selection has been met with a certain degree of controversy, as many considered it a gimmick song, and not worthy of representing Spain. It has also met controversy because Rodolfo Chikilicuatre is a comedic act, with no prior songs, and was backed by a private show (Buenafuente) and a private TV station (LaSexta). RTVE stands by their choice of voting system.

On March 11, 2008, Rodolfo announced some changes to the lyrics of his song to comply with the rules of the Eurovision Song Contest, thus removing partially the names of the politicians included in the song (José Luis Rodríguez Zapatero, Hugo Chávez and Mariano Rajoy). Even if Chávez's name was completely removed, a reference to a previous incident with the king Juan

Carlos I of Spain was kept. A non-political reference to Serbia was added. The song was also made longer, as the original was considered too short, going from 1:20 to 2:56 minutes, and several verses in English were added. The new version was presented on March 14, 2008.

He has sung the "Chiki-Chiki" theme with other performers: King Africa, Tata Golosa and Dustin the Turkey.

During the final contest of the Eurovision 2008 on May 24, 2008, the song "Chiki-Chiki" reached sixteenth place with 55 points, together with Albania.

Source (edited): "http://en.wikipedia.org/wiki/Rodolfo_Chikilicuatre"

Rosa Maria Sardà

Rosa María Sardà (Barcelona, 1941) is a Spanish actress and comedian.

She has played roles in Spanish and Catalan. She was married to the comedian Josep Maria Mainat (a member of the group La Trinca), and she's Xavier Sardà's elder sister. She started in 1970s and has become one of the most important actresses of Spanish cinema and theatre.

Filmography

- 2003 *Te doy mis ojos*
- 2002 *A mi madre le gustan las mujeres*
- 2002 *Deseo*
- 2002 *Dos tipos duros*
- 2002 *El embrujo de Shangai*
- 2002 *El viaje de Carol*
- 2001 *Sin vergüenza*
- 2001 *Torrente 2, misión en Marbella*
- 2000 *Anita no pierde el tren*
- 1999 *Todo sobre mi madre*
- 1998 *Amic/Amat*
- 1998 *La niña de tus ojos*
- 1998 *Mátame mucho*
- 1997 *Airbag*
- 1997 *Carícies*
- 1997 *Grandes ocasiones*
- 1997 *Siempre hay un camino a la derecha*
- 1996 *Actrius*
- 1996 *La duquesa roja*
- 1995 *El efecto mariposa*
- 1995 *Pareja de tres*
- 1995 *Suspiros de España (y Portugal)*
- 1994 *Alegre ma non troppo*
- 1994 *El hundimiento del Titanic*
- 1994 *Enciende mi pasión*
- 1994 *Escenas de una orgía en Formentera*
- 1993 *El cianuro... ¿sólo o con leche?*
- 1992 *¿Por qué lo llaman amor cuando quieren decir sexo?*
- 1992 *La fiebre del oro*
- 1991 *Ho sap, el ministre?*
- 1990 *Rateta, rateta*
- 1990 *Un submarí a les tovalles*
- 1987 *Moros y cristianos*
- 1980 *El vicario de Olot*

Theatre

- 2004: *Witt*
- 1982: *Yo me bajo el la próxima ¿y usted?*
- 1982: *Duet per a violet*

Main prizes

- 1994 Goya Award Best Supporting Actress for *¿Por qué lo llaman amor cuando quieren decir sexo?*
- 2002 Goya Award Best Supporting Actress for *Sin vergüenza*
- 2003: Fotogramas de Plata
- 2001: Unión de Actores
- 2001: Mar del Plata Film Festival Mención Especial for *Anita no pierde el tren*

Source (edited): "http://en.wikipedia.org/wiki/Rosa_Maria_Sard%C3%A0"

Secun de la Rosa

Secun de la Rosa (Barcelona, December 23, 1969) is a Spanish actor and theatre author and director.

He studied drama in Cristina Rota's atelier, and although he's popular thanks to his humorist roles in cinema and TV, he has worked as author-director in several theatrical production. He has been awarded and nominated for these plays and he has also received the 2003 *Premio al mejor actor de la Unión de Actores* as an actor.

Filmography

Feature film

- *Casual day* (2007) by Max Lemcke.
- *Encerrados en la mina* by David Serrano.
- *El síndrome de Svensson* (2006) by Kepa Sojo.
- *Los dos lados de la cama* (2005) by Emilio Martínez Lázaro.
- *Las aventuras de Pocholo y Borjamari* (2004) by Juan Cabestany, Enrique Lavigne.
- *El chocolate del loro* (2004) by Ernesto Martín.
- *Hay motivo* (2004) by Joaquín Oristrell.
- *Incautos* (2004) by Miguel Bardem.
- *Los abajo firmantes* (2003) by Joaquín Oristrell.
- *Días de fútbol* (2003) by David Serrano.
- *El otro lado de la cama* (2002) by Emilio Martínez Lázaro.
- *Noche de reyes* by Miguel Bardem.
- *Peor imposible* (2002) by José Semprúm/David Blanco.
- *Aunque tú no lo sepas* (2000) by J.V. Cordova.
- *Me da igual* (2000) by David Gordon.
- *Vadene via* by Max Vianchi, Ana Pamplons

Short films

- *Desaliñada* (2001) by Gustavo Salmerón.
- *Postales de la India* (2000) by Juanjo Díaz Polo.
- *Al rojo vivo* by Raúl Muñoz.

TV

- *Los irrepetibles*, La Sexta

- *Aída*, Telecinco
- *Paco y Veva*, TVE
- *7 vidas*, Telecinco
- *Cuéntame cómo pasó*, TVE
- *El grupo*, Telecinco
- *Policías* Telecinco
- *Compañeros,* Antena 3

Theatre
- *El rincón de la borracha* by Secun de la Rosa.
- *Los openheart* by Andrés Lima.
- *Pensar amb els ulls* by Joan Brossa.
- *Radio para,* by Secun de la Rosa.
- *Obededor* by Amparo Valle.
- *El homosexual de Copi* by Gustavo Tambascio.
- *Lorca* Cía. Lluis Pascual.
- *Susrealismos* Cía. Caracalva.
- *Te odio* by Juanjo Díaz Polo.
- *A las tantas* by Secun de la Rosa.
- *Anoche por poco sueño contigo*, Cía. Caracalva
- *Bola de sebo* Alberto San Juan, Cía. Animalario .
- *Oración*, Fernando Arrabal Cía. Madera 17.
- *Esperando al zurdo*, by Cristina Rota.

Source (edited): "http://en.wikipedia.org/wiki/Secun_de_la_Rosa"

Señor Wences

Wenceslao Moreno (April 17, 1896 – April 20, 1999), better known as **Señor Wences**, was a Spanish ventriloquist. His popularity grew with his frequent appearances on CBS-TV's *Ed Sullivan Show* in the 1950s and '60s.

Early life

Wences was born in Peñaranda de Bracamonte, Salamanca, Spain. His father was Antonio Moreno Ross, artist, and his mother was Josefa Centeno Lavera, both from Salamanca. His name Wenceslao is of Czech origin (Václav) meaning "victorious". As a newborn, his family was so destitute that his birth certificate was three days late being filed. (This has led to some confusion regarding Moreno's age at death.)

Career

Wences was known for his speed, skill, and grace as a ventriloquist. His stable of characters included Johnny, a childlike face drawn on Wences' hand, which he would place atop an otherwise headless doll and with whom Wences conversed while switching his voices between Johnny's falsetto and his own voice at amazing speed. Wences would create Johnny's face on stage to open his act, placing his thumb next to, and in front of, his bent first finger; the first finger would be the upper lip, and the thumb the lower lip. He used lipstick to draw the lips onto the respective fingers and then drew eyes onto the upper part of the first finger, finishing the effect with a tiny long-haired wig on top of his hand. Flexing the thumb would move the "lips."

Another popular Wences character was the gruff-voiced Pedro, a disembodied head in a box. Wences was forced to suddenly invent the character when his regular, full-sized dummy was destroyed during a 1936 train accident en route to Chicago. Pedro would either 'speak' from within the closed box, or speak with moving lips — simply growling, "s'awright" ("it's all right") — when Wences opened the box's front panel with his free hand. A large part of Wences' comedy lay in the well-timed, high-speed exchange of words between himself and his creations, and in the difference in their voice pitches.

Part of Wences's act involved the ventriloquist throwing his voice while his mouth was otherwise engaged (smoking or drinking). Another favorite prop was a telephone, with Wences playing both sides of a telephone conversation. For the "caller" he simulated a "filtered" voice as it would sound over a telephone wire. This voice always began a conversation with a shouted "Moreno?" (Wences's true surname), with Wences in person patiently explaining, "No, Moreno is not here."

Wences usually built to a big finish that combined ventriloquism with juggling and plate-spinning. As Wences performed his routines, Pedro and Johnny mercilessly heckled him with flawless comedic timing.

Although he was an international favorite for decades, his main career was made in the United States, where he arrived in 1934 or 1935. In addition to live performances at nightclubs, he appeared regularly on TV variety shows, especially his 48 frequent appearances on CBS's *Ed Sullivan Show*; on Broadway; in Las Vegas casino theatres; and in feature films. Much later in his career he was introduced to a new generation of fans on *The Muppet Show*. His last TV appearance was on *The Very Best of the Ed Sullivan Show, #2*, a retrospective in which nonagenarian Wences talked about "Suliban" and performed a brief spot of ventriloquism.

Wences pronounced his name the traditional Castilian way, which in English sounds like "WEN-thess". After Sullivan would announce him saying his name as "Señor Wen-sess", the ventriloquist would subtly correct Sullivan's pronunciation by announcing himself to the audience: "Hello, I am Señor Wenthess".

In the early 1980s, a Tri-State Honda dealer's commercial featured Señor Wences with Johnny. Pedro's "s'awright" was a voice from the tricked out glovebox. Señor Wences would point out all of the car's features to which Johnny would reply, "Nice!" This may have been Señor Wences final commercial appearance. It was shot in Puerto Rico because its star declined to travel to New York.

Catchphrases

One of Wences's trademark bits of shtick (referenced several times below) involves his dialogue with a low voice emanating from inside a box. At the opening of the dialogue he would shout, "Hello in the box!" At the conclusion of the dialogue, he would open the lid of the box and ask "S'awright?" ("It's all right?") and the box voice would answer "S'awriiight!"

Another involved explaining to his hand puppet Johnny that something was easy (or difficult) to do, to which the puppet would reply the contrary, such as, "Easy for you, for me ees very deefeecult!" in his Spanish accent.

These catchphrases were incorporated into a record Wences released in 1959 by Joy Records, featuring the songs "S-All Right? S-All Right" and "Deefeecult For You-Easy For Me."

Death and legacy

Wences received the Lifetime Achievement Award from the US National Comedy Hall of Fame in 1996.

Despite his retirement by age 100, Wences' famous puppets Johnny and Pedro "continued working". Ventriloquist Michele LaFong performed at Wences' 100th birthday celebration at New York's Friars Club (where he was made a lifetime member), and he was so impressed that he befriended LaFong. Not only did he give her his puppets, but also taught her how to perform his classic routines. Las Vegas headliner LaFong is the only ventriloquist authorized by the Wences Estate to perform Johnny and Pedro, plus Wences' routines.

Wences died just after his 103rd birthday. He had been residing in New York City's Upper West Side on 54th Street, just around the corner from the Ed Sullivan Theater. That section of 54th Street has been named Señor Wences Way. His portrait can be seen at the Players Club in New York.

Personal life

Wences married Esperanza Martin (1902–1983); for her he named Johnny as "Johnny Martin." His second and last wife, Natalie Cover, née Eisler (1917–2005) was also his manager. His first wife was born in North Africa, and the second was born in Russia. His nephew José Luis Moreno and brother Felipe Moreno were also ventriloquists. Wences has a a son in Chile and a granddaughter Marcela Moreno in the US.

- At the end of a 1959 episode of the cartoon series *Quick Draw McGraw*, Quick Draw McGraw and his sidekick Baba Looey repeat the famous lines of "S'awriiight".
- In "Family Portrait", a Season 1 episode of the television series *The Munsters*, Herman Munster lifts a manhole cover while looking for Grandpa. He yells down the manhole, and a voice replies that Grandpa is not there. Herman says, "OK" and the voice repeats, "OK." Herman says "S'awright?" and the voice responds "S'awright."
- In "Hassle in the Castle", an early episode of the animated Hanna-Barbera series *Scooby-Doo, Where Are You!*, his voice and catch phrase "S'awriiight" is used by the talking skeleton head that gives Shaggy directions.
- Another Hanna-Barbera homage can be found in "By Rollercoaster to Upsan Downs", an episode of *Wacky Races*, in which one of The Slag Brothers raises the hood of a car to ask "S'awright?", to which a voice from under the hood gives the obligatory answer.
- Several episodes of the animated series *Roger Ramjet* are set in the fictional South American republic of San Domino, which is so small and impoverished that the President's Cabinet is an actual wooden cabinet. When the President wishes confirmation of some train of thought, he asks it, "S'awright?" and a gruff voice from within gives the familiar answer.
- In the 1965 *Chilly Willy* cartoon "Half-Baked Alaska", while getting his order for pancakes from Smedly the dog, Chilly and Smedly did a routine similar to the "Nice? Nice" act. A similar gag happens at the end of "Pesty Guest", produced that same year.
- In the 1979 movie *The In-Laws*, a South American dictator speaks to the protagonists indirectly, via a "Johnny"-like character drawn on his hand named "Señor Pepe." At that point, any doubts they may have had about his sanity are confirmed.
- In "Fat Butt and Pancake Head", a 2003 episode of the animated television series *South Park*, Eric Cartman creates a hand puppet in the style of Señor Wences' Johnny. Cartman's puppet is a parody of singer Jennifer Lopez, but the puppet still speaks like Johnny, with a high-pitched voice and stereotypical Spanish accent. Cartman and the puppet also go through several of Señor Wences's classic routines, such as having the puppet "kiss" a real person. Cartman and "Miss Lopez" share the trademark "s'awright" routine Wences used to do with his "Pedro" puppet.
- In Disney's *Aladdin*, there are two references to Señor Wences. The first happens when Aladdin first meets the Genie, (Robin Williams) who describing himself as "often imitated", employs a dummy and a high-pitched, Spanish-accented voice similar to Johnny. The second is near the end of the film, when Aladdin suggests Jafar wish to be a genie. The Genie makes a Johnny-like hand puppet.
- In Disney's *Return of Jafar*, Genie sings "There's Nothing in the World like a Friend", during which he uses a high-pitched, Spanish-accented voice during the line, "Moroccans set my fairy tales of seven veils".
- In the *Sam & Max* comic book, *Bad Day on the Moon*, Max spends a brief time as disembodied spirit in possession of Sam's hand, taking on the appearance of a Johnny-type puppet, except with bunny ears, and saying the "S'awright" line.
- In the novel *Caramelo*, one of the characters meets Señor Wences in a Chicago jail cell.
- In the movie *America's Sweethearts*, when Lee Phillips (Billy Crystal) urges Dave Kingman (Stanley Tucci) that they have to make a film with an actor that Phillips insists is a genius, Kingman responds, "No, there's only one genius in this business, and that was Señor Wences. A little lipstick, some hair, and his hand, and the guy had a

career for 85 years!"
- In the online game *Kingdom of Loathing* speaking to the character Blaine, whose icon is a box, will initiate certain quests. However, if he has no quests to give the player, the description will read, "You knock on the side of the crate, and ask 'S'alright?' A voice inside mutters, 'S'alright.'"
- On the July 14, 2009 episode of *The Colbert Report*, host Stephen Colbert used a Johnny-like character named *Senator* Wences to question Supreme Court nominee Sonia Sotomayor during her confirmation hearing.
- In "The Mail Goes to Jail", the February 7, 1985 episode of the sitcom *Cheers*, Dianne is trapped in a heating duct under the floor of the bar and only her head is visible from the vent. Sam gets up to call someone to get her out, closes the vent, and then opens it again to ask, "S'alwright?", to which she quickly responds "S'awriiiight".
- In "Gone", a sixth season episode of the action TV series *Buffy the Vampire Slayer*, Buffy is made invisible. While invisible she holds up a skull and makes it says "S'awright".
- In the May 20, 2010 *The Rush Limbaugh Show*, Limbaugh derisively referred to the President of Mexico, Felipe Calderón, as Senor Weñces and gave a short review of who Señor Wences is. Limbaugh explained the comparison as Calderón seemed to be a puppet, articulating US President Barack Obama's philosophies during the State visit press conference on May 19, 2010.
- In "For Those Who Think Young", the second season premiere of the cable TV series *Mad Men*, Paul Kinsey arrives at the Sterling Cooper conference room for a meeting with the firm's creative team, and opens and shuts his briefcase, saying, "s'awriiiight", a la Pedro.
- In the season three episode of Mystery Science Theater 3000 "Pod People", a character in the movie being watched is locked inside a trailer. Crow T. Robot comments on this by quoting the "S'alwright in the box?", "S'alwright" routine.
- In the Ray Stevens music video *The Skies Just Ain't Friendly Anymore*, Stevens visually mimics a hand puppet in the same manner of a Senòr Wences character.

Source (edited): "http://en.wikipedia.org/wiki/Se%C3%B1or_Wences"

Vital Aza

Vital Aza Álvarez-Buylla (25 April 1851 – 13 December 1912) was a Spanish author, playwright, poet and satirist, born in Pola de Lena, Asturias, northwestern Spain. After studying and practicing medicine, he began to write plays, some with Miguel Ramos Carrión. His first, *Basta de matemáticas*, which premiered at the Variedades in 1874, was highly successful and was followed by more than 70 other plays. The centenary of his birth was celebrated by Aguilar's publication of an anthology of Aza's best plays in the Colección Crisol (1951).

Source (edited): "http://en.wikipedia.org/wiki/Vital_Aza"

Yolanda Ramos

Yolanda Ramos (Barcelona, September 4, 1968) is a Spanish comedian actress and scriptwriter.

She has taken part in several shows of the theatre groups El Terrat and La cubana. In the last years, she has become very popular thanks to her impersonations in *Homo Zapping* and her role of a TV conductor in *Volver* (2006). She wrote the script of the advertising campaign of ONCE in 2000.

TV

- El intermedio
- 7 Vidas (2006)
- Buenafuente (2005)
- Homo Zapping(2003-2005)
- Los más (2005)
- Vitamina N (2002-2004)
- Me lo dijo Pérez (1999)

Source (edited): "http://en.wikipedia.org/wiki/Yolanda_Ramos"

Ángel Garó

Ángel Garó (La Línea de la Concepción, January 12, 1965) is a Spanish actor and comedian.

He became very popular in the 1990s thanks to his performances in *Un, dos, tres* and his show *Personas humanas*. He dubbed all the characters of the movie *FernGully: The Last Rainforest* in Spain, and he has taken part in different programs like *Noche de Fiesta* or *Mira quien baila*.

Source (edited): "http://en.wikipedia.org/wiki/%C3%81ngel_Gar%C3%B3"

Ángel Martín

Ángel Martín Gómez (Barcelona, October 5, 1977) is an actor, a TV presenter, comedian, and screenwriter.

Beginnings

He studied piano in Barcelona and worked with his father playing music for old people. He spent the money he earned to pay for his studies in an acting academy.

Television

He attended an audition for the TV channel Paramount Comedy where the producer was looking for new talent. He put a sheet over his head and spoke about the disadvantages of being a ghost. He passed the audition, and afterwards, joined the group of comedians already at the channel, writing and performing his monologues in the programme *Nuevos Cómicos (New comedians)* Some of them are:

Leyendas Urbanas *[Urban Legends]*,
Cuentos Infantiles *[Children's Stories]*
Sexo y Milagros *[Sex and Miracles]*

Ángel collaborated on **Noche sin tregua** *[Night without truce]*, his friend Dani Mateo's TV show on Paramount Comedy, and also on **La Noche con Fuentes & Cía** *[Night with Fuentes & Cía]* with Manel Fuentes.

He was one of the screenwriters of the successful series *7 Vidas* [7 lives].

He worked from March 2006 to January 2011 at La Sexta, co-presenting *Sé lo que hicisteis...* [I know what you did...], a humorous programme which takes a critical look at the world of celebrity and sensationalist TV programmes with Patricia Conde.

Cinema

Ángel Martín has written scripts for many short films.

He appeared in *Pernambuco*, directed by Albert Ponte and *Marta Molina*, by Javier Ocaña.

Theatre

He was in the play *¡Qué viene Richi!* (*The Nerd*) by Larry Shoe, in Madrid (Spain).

Awards

- 2007

- 'Man of the year' (Men's health magazine) - 'Comedian of the year' (Jaja Festival in Zaragoza) - 'Best Light Entertainment Presenters: Ángel Martín and Patricia Conde' (ATV 2006) - 'Best Light Entertainment Presenter' (TP de Oro 2007)

- 2008

- 'Best Light Entertainment Presenter' (TP de Oro 2008)
Source (edited): "http://en.wikipedia.org/wiki/%C3%81ngel_Mart%C3%ADn"

El Jueves

El Jueves (Spanish for "*The Thursday*") is a Spanish satirical weekly magazine published in Barcelona. Its complete title is "El Jueves, la revista que sale los Miércoles" ("*The Thursday, the magazine that comes out on Wednesdays*"). As of 2007, one issue costs 2.50 € in mainland Spain and Balearic Islands and 2.70 € in the Canary Islands.

Layout

Founded in 1977, it has currently between 72 and 80 pages, with about 20 pages about current political, economical or social affairs, always in an irreverent tone and in comic format. The rest are weekly strips. An extra is edited every three months with between 104 and 120 pages about a particular issue: monarchy, religion, videogames or some piece of news related to those or other topics. The magazine has had more than 1,500 issues. Its mascot is the jester that appears since the beginning on the ffront page.

Some of the recurring sections of El Jueves are:
- "Te lo juro News", a four-page newspaper parody with comic strips, brief humorous texts and photomontages about current national and international affairs.
- "Recortes de la prensa seria", a section with News of the Weird-like headlines or curiosities published in ordinary press.
- "El gilipollas de la semana", about the most ridiculous person of the week according to the El Jueves contributors.
- "En familia", letters to the editor.
- A poster, generally by Vizcarra.
- The editorial about the current affairs topic that is developed in the first pages of the magazine.

Supplements

With the issue about United States (number 1428), another magazine was published, Mister K, which addresses children and teenagers.

In 2003, *El Jueves Campus* was first published, a supplement to 20 minutos with several comic strips that focused on students. It is distributed for free on the second Thursday of every month in university areas.

Seizure for insults to the Crown

The July 18, 2007 edition of the magazine was sequestered by law on July 20, for an alleged violation of laws 490.3 and 491 on insults to the Crown, since the Prince of Asturias and his wife, who were portrayed with a caricature on the front cover performing a sexual act. This cartoon referred to a new proposal of the government, where €2,500 will be given to parents for each newborn child. As the Prince has never held a paid job, the caption said that if the Princess got pregnant and they got the money, it's the closest he would ever come to working. The magazine's website was also briefly closed, but has since re-opened. On November 13, 2007, Guillermo Torres and Manel Fontdevila were found guilty of having offended the crown by vilifying "the crown in the most gratuitous and unnecessary way". They were fined €3,000 each.

Reporters without borders discussed the condemnation as the first of those that declared that "slightly curtailed" freedom of the press in Spain for year 2007. The magazine and the journalists appealed to the Constitutional Court of Spain, which, declaring that "has not been proven that the matter is not of constitutional significance," refused to hear the appeal, thus confirming the sentence. The magazine announced that it will bring the case to the European Court of Human Rights, declaring to want to make clear that neither Torres nor Fontdevilla, the two authors, committed a crime, and added "we know it's a long path, but it's necessary to accomplish that the justice declares that a magazine cannot be seized."
Source (edited): "http://en.wikipedia.org/wiki/El_Jueves"

Generation of '27

The **Generation of '27** (Spanish: *Generación del 27*) was an influential group of poets that arose in Spanish literary circles between 1923 and 1927, essentially out of a shared desire to experience and work with avant-garde forms of art and poetry. Their first formal meeting took place in Seville in 1927 to mark the 300th anniversary of the death of the baroque poet Luis de Góngora. Writers and intellectuals celebrated an homage in the *Ateneo de Sevilla*, which retrospectively became the foundational act of the movement.

Terminology

The name of "generation" has been discussed. The Generation of '27 has also been called, with lesser success, "Generation of the Dictatorship", "Generation of the Republic", "Generation Guillén-Lorca" (Guillén being its oldest author, and Lorca its youngest), "Generation of 1925" (average publishing date of the first book of each author), "Generation of Avant-Guardes", "Generation of Friendship," etc. According to Petersen, "generation group" or a "constellation" are better terms which are not so much historically restricted as "generation."

Aesthetic style

The Generation of '27 cannot be neatly categorized stylistically, due to wide variety of genres and styles cultivated by its members. While some members, such as Jorge Guillén, wrote in a style that has been loosely called jubilant and joyous and celebrates the instant, others, such as Rafael Alberti, underwent a poetic evolution which led him from youthful poetry of a more romantic vein to politically engaged verses later in life.

The group tried to bridge the gap between Spanish popular culture and folklore, classical literary tradition and European avant-guardes. It evolved from pure poetry which emphasized music in poetry, in the vein of Baudelaire, to Futurism, Cubism, Ultraist and Creationism, to become influenced by Surrealism and finally to disperse in interior and exterior exile following the Civil War and World War II (sometimes gathered by historians under the term of the "European Civil War"). The Generation of '27 made a frequent use of visionary images, free verses and the so-called impure poetry preconized by Pablo Neruda.

Members

In a restrictive sense, the Generation of '27 refers to ten authors, Jorge Guillén, Pedro Salinas, Rafael Alberti, Federico García Lorca, Dámaso Alonso, Gerardo Diego, Luis Cernuda, Vicente Aleixandre, Manuel Altolaguirre and Emilio Prados. However, many others were in their orbit, some olders such as Fernando Villalón, José Moreno Villa or León Felipe and Nathan Manuel Rudolph, and others youngers such as Miguel Hernández. Others have been forgotten by the critics, such as Juan Larre, Pepe Alameda, Mauricio Bacarisse, Juan José Domenchina, José María Hinojosa, José Bergamín or Juan Gil-Albert. There is also the "Other generation of '27," a term coined by José López Rubio, formed by himself and humorist disciples of Ramón Gómez de la Serna, including: Enrique Jardiel Poncela, Edgar Neville, Miguel Mihura and Antonio de Lara, "Tono", writers who would integrate after the Civil War (1936-39) the editing board of *La Codorniz*...

Furthermore, the Generation of '27, as clearly reflected in the literary press of the period, was not exclusively restricted to poets, including artists such as Luis Buñuel, the caricaturist K-Hito, the surrealist painters Salvador Dalí and Óscar Domínguez, the painter and sculptor Maruja Mallo, as well as Benjamín Palencia, Gregorio Prieto, Manuel Ángeles Ortiz and Gabriel García Maroto, the toreros Ignacio Sánchez Mejías, Rodolfo Halffter and Jesús Bal y Gay, musicologists and composers belonging to the Group of Eight, including Bal and Gay, Ernesto Halffter and his brother Rodolfo, Juan José Mantecón, Julián Bautista, Fernando Remacha, Rosa García Ascot, Salvador Bacarisse and Gustavo Pittaluga. There was also the Catalan Group who presented themselves in 1931 under the name of *Grupo de Artistas Catalanes Independientes*, including Roberto Gerhard, Baltasar Samper, Manuel Blancafort, Ricardo Lamote de Grignon, Eduardo Toldrá and Federico Mompou.

Finally, not all literary works were written in Spanish: Salvador Dalí and Óscar Domínguez also wrote in French, while Felipe Alfau wrote in English. Foreigners such as the Chilean poets Pablo Neruda and Vicente Huidobro, the Argentine writer Jorge Luis Borges, and the Franco-Spanish painter Francis Picabia also shared a lot with the aesthetics of the Generation of '27.

The Generation of '27 was not exclusively located in Madrid, but rather deployed itself in a geographical constellation which maintained links together. The most important nucleus were in Sevilla, around the *Mediodía* review, Tenerife around the *Gaceta de Arte* and Málaga, around the *Litoral* review. Others members resided in Galicia, Catalonia and Valladolid.

The Currents of '27

The Generation of '27 was not a homogeneous group, and have been frequently classed in couples or trios. Rafael Alberti and Federico García Lorca thus formed the Neopopular group, which tried to approach the poetry of Gil Vicente and of the Gypsie *Romancero*, or the *Lírica cancioneril*. These were particularly intent upon founding the roots of their poetry in popular folklore.

Jorge Guillén, influenced by Paul Valéry's pure poetry, and Pedro Salinas, the great poet of love of '27, were two philology teachers.

The Surrealist group was larger, and included in particular the Nobel Prize Vicente Aleixandre, probably the most creative of all and one of the most influential poets of his generation in the second half of the 20th century, as well as Luis Cernuda, who lived Surrealism as a revelation which permitted him to assume his homosexual desire, and who constitute the first Spanish-language "poet of experience" in the Anglo-Saxon sense of the word. Others poets of '27 influenced by Surrealism include Rafael Alberti, Federico García Lorca in his *Llanto por Ignacio Sánchez Mejías*, *Poeta en Nueva York* and *Sonetos del amor oscuro*; José María Hinojosa with his *La flor de Califórnia* (with the accent on the i) and Emilio Prados.

Along with Manuel Altolaguirre, Emilio Prados constituted the young group of Málaga around the *Litoral* review published by Altolaguirre.

The Spanish Civil War and its aftermaths

The Civil War brought about the splitting of the movement: García Lorca was murdered, Miguel Hernandez died in jail, and other members (Rafael Alberti, Jose Bergamin, Leon Felipe, Luis Cernuda, Pedro Salinas, Juan Ramón Jiménez, Bacarisse) were forced into exile, although virtually all kept writing and publishing late into the 20th century.

Dámaso Alonso and Gerardo Diego were among those who reluctantly remained in Spain after the Francoists' victory, and more or less reached agreements with the new authoritarian and traditionalist regime, or even openly supported it in the case of Diego. The latter evolved a lot, combining tradition and avant-guarde, and mixing many different themes, from toreo to music to religious and existentialism disquiets, landscapes, etc. Others, such as Juan Gil-Albert, simply ignored the new regime, taking the path of interior exile and *de facto* converting themselves in guides and masters of a new generation of poets, such as Vicente Aleixandre.

However, for many Spaniards the harsh reality of Francoist Spain and its reactionary nature meant that the cerebral and aesthetic verses of the Generation of '27 did not connect with what was truly happening, a task that was handled more capably by the poets of the **Generation of '50** and the social poets.

Source (edited): "http://en.wikipedia.org/wiki/Generation_of_%2727"

José Luis Torrente

José Luis Torrente is a fictional character created by Spanish actor and director Santiago Segura and the main character in the *Torrente* dark comedy-action film series. The series so far includes three films; *Torrente: El brazo tonto de la ley* (1998), *Torrente 2: Misión en Marbella* (2001), *Torrente 3: El protector* (2005) plus the forthcoming Torrente 4. There are videogames *Torrente: El videojuego* and *Torrente 3*, which were released with the second and third movies, respectively. [(And by other part, the pornographic film-copyryght *Torrente X: Operación Vinagra* (2005) and *Torrente X 2: Misión en Torrelavega* (2006), too].

Description and Career

Born and usually resident in Madrid, Spain, José Luis Torrente is an ugly, bald, overweight, dirty, corrupt, lying, fascist, racist, chauvinistic and anticommunist retired cop. He refuses to accept his expulsion from the Police corps, so he still "patrols" each night in his old car in order to "fight" what he considers criminal actions. Poor immigrants and drug-addicts are often victims of his actions, while he usually refuses to confront real criminals due to his actual cowardice (sometimes, however, Torrente is able to show a surprising amount of courage). Torrente openly states his admiration for *Generalissimo* Francisco Franco (and later for King Juan Carlos and the crown prince), and is a declared fan of the Atlético de Madrid Football Club and Spanish singer *El Fary*.

Following his discharge, he loses his partner (an old mentor) in a shoot-out in ChinaTown brothel. He had a depressive disorder and was dismissed from his job as a cop. Due to his lack of a proper job (he continues patrolling and undertaking detective work), Torrente faces financial problems from time to time and lives in a dirty small apartment in a depressing part of the city. He used to live with his old and sick father Felipe (later revealed to be actually Torrente's uncle, due to an affair between Felipe's wife and his twin brother Mauricio) and forced him to beg for food and money in the streets, spending almost all the money collected plus his social security annuity in his personal affairs. Felipe is not the only one manipulated by Torrente in order to achieve his own goals.

Mission in Marbella

Torrente accidentally discovers and destroys a drug dealing maffia which uses a Chinese restaurant as cover, only to steal their money and start a new life as new rich in Torremolinos. He spends then millions in the Spanish Mediterranean coast until he loses all his money in a casino in Marbella. There, he establishes himself as a private investigator, discovers that his real father is the local crime boss Mauricio Torrente and stops the James Bond-type supervillain Spinelli from destroying the city - throwing his super-missile over the British naval base at Gibraltar instead. Due to this action Torrente receives a medal and is permitted to join the Police again as a traffic cop in Madrid.

Bodyguard

In *El Protector*, Torrente is ordered to act as the personal bodyguard of Eurodeputy Giannina Ricci, which is targeted by a powerful corporation which dislikes her environmental policies. The decision is actually the result of a secret agreement between the company itself and corrupt elements within the upper levels of the National Police: as Torrente is the worst agent in the whole country, everybody expects that the assassination attempt will be easy. Torrente and his men, however, are able to save Ricci and later flee to the United States, where they accidentally kill US President George W. Bush. During his last mission Torrente mets for the first time his secret son, Torrente Junior, who is presumably the result of relations of Torrente with an unknown woman.

Coming to the US?

Santiago Segura has said several times that there will be more Torrente movies if they still do well at the (Spanish) box office. The idea of making a remake in the United States was offered for the first time in 2002 by US filmmaker Oliver Stone, who suggested Josh Brolin and mainly to Robert de Niro for the lead role. Stone had seen the first two movies during a film festival in Europe and declared his admiration for the character, meeting Segura and befriending him. This first negotiations, however, didn't end well, but the rights to make a US version were finally purchased by New Line Cinema in 2006 and two American writers, Mike Bender and Doug Chernack, were hired to draw a first version of the script. It has not been revealed if the new movie would be a real remake, in which the new Torrente will be a US version of the Spanish one, or a movie featuring a mission of the horrendous Spanish policeman on US soil. In any case, it seems that Segura will not repeat in the role if there is any US version.

Famous people´s cameos

- Javier Bardem: Torrente, el brazo tonto de la ley.
- Jorge Sanz: Torrente, el brazo tonto de la ley.
- John Landis: Torrente 3: el Protector.
- Oliver Stone: Torrente 3: el Protector.
- Guillermo del Toro: Torrente 3: el Protector.
- Iker Casillas: Torrente 3: el Protector.
- Gonzalo Higuaín: Torrente 4: Lethal Chrisis (Crisis Letal).
- Sergio Agüero: Torrente 4: Lethal Chrisis (Crisis Letal).
- Sergio Ramos: Torrente 4: Lethal Chrisis (Crisis Letal).

Source (edited): "http://en.wikipedia.org/wiki/Jos%C3%A9_Luis_Torrente"

7 vidas

7 Vidas is a Spanish sitcom which aired on Telecinco from 1999 to 2006. Its title translates as "7 lives" and the symbol of the sitcom is a cat, in reference to the belief that cats have 7 lives (curiously two lives less than cats from English-speaking countries which are popularly considered to have nine lives). The series is to date 2006 the longest running show of all-time in the history of Spanish television.

It was originally inspired by the American blockbuster Friends.

At its start it wasn't a great audience success, but over time, the show continued and gained more and more popularity season after season, making it the most popular Spanish TV series of all time.

It was in *7 Vidas* that the now internationally famous actress Paz Vega, and other Spanish actors first became household names in Spain.

The sitcom tells the story of a group of friends in Madrid. David (Toni Cantó) was in a coma for more than 18 years and suddenly awakes and starts discovering the new world in which he lives. His neighbour, Sole (Amparo Baró) is an old woman with a penchant for slapping anyone who behaves in a way she dislikes round the back of the neck. Sole soon becomes one of the show's most popular characters. Other characters were Sole's sexually frustrated son, Paco (Javier Cámara), Carlota (Blanca Portillo) David's single sister and Laura (Laurita to her friends) (Paz Vega), their cousin from Seville (with her colourful Sevillian accent), initially Paco's principal love interest and then David's.

Characters came and went, and by the end of the sitcom the only character who had appeared in the first chapter and lasted until its end was Sole. Other long-standing characters, and the two most popular, in addition to Sole, were Gonzalo (Gonzalo de Castro), a waiter who later became a main character and Carlota's husband (although they were later divorced), and Diana (Anabel Alonso), a frustrated actress, and a naïve lesbian. She was the first homosexual character in Spanish television who didn't follow stereotypes.

The script of the show was well-known for poking fun at current events, politicians and celebrities and often contained a lot of risqué jokes.

Often scenes of the sitcom were set in Gonzalo's café, the "Kasi Ke No" - just as many *Friends* scenes were set in the *Central Perk* café - Sole's house and Carlota's house, and many outside shots were also used.

By the end of its run, the show was totally different from Friends.

7 Vidas was also known for its multiple cameos of famous people, including Shakira, El Canto del Loco, politician Santiago Carrillo, and footballer Samuel Eto'o. Hugh Grant was pencilled in to appear in one chapter, but the actor subsequently declined the offer.

By the time the show reached its final episode *7 Vidas* had clocked up 204 chapters, with a macro celebration featuring all of the 19 main characters who had appeared over the series' history, including a video from Paz Vega who was busy filming in the United States and was unable to appear in person. A live interpretation of the main theme was also performed by El Canto del Loco, a Spanish pop group. That chapter was recorded and transmitted live without interruptions, bar a few minutes for commercials, which were used to change clothes and represent the passing of the time.

ANT1 channel in Greece picked up the rights to 7 Vidas for a Greek remake of the show, premiering in its fall 2008 lineup and entitled "7 Ζωές" (7 Lives).

Spin-off Aída

The popularity of "7 vidas" led in 2005 to a spin-off, Aída, still running as of 2010. It featured a later popular "7 vidas" character of the same name, known for her vulgarity and for representing a "typical" working class Spanish woman. The series was set in a new context, with entirely new characters, though some characters from "7 vidas" appeared in some episodes, and others, mentioned in "7 vidas" but never shown were introduced as regulars of the new show. In 2009, when Carmen Machi, the actress who played Aída, left the series, new characters appeared and now the series continues under the same basic premise.

Source (edited): "http://en.wikipedia.org/wiki/7_vidas"

Abdelaziz (TV series)

Abdelaziz is an Algerian-Spanish situation comedy that originally aired on September 24, 2007. The show features the adventures and misadventures of president Abdelaziz Bouteflika (played by himself), along with his friends, family and acquaintances. The entire nation was hugely surprised by the fact that it was Abdelaziz himself who played the main role in the show (this case was similar to Hugo Chávez's talk show, Aló Presidente) and many of his catchphrases (like *"May the Christian God damn it to hell!"*) have become part of the popular culture lexicon.

Source (edited): "http://en.wikipedia.org/wiki/Abdelaziz_(TV_series)"

Aquí no hay quien viva

Aquí no hay quien viva (Spanish, 'No One Could Live Here' or, translated more freely, 'This Place is Awful') is a Spanish television comedy focusing on the inhabitants of the fictional building in *Desengaño 21, Calle Desengaño* being a street between the Districts of Gran Via and Chueca in Madrid. The episodes debuted on the Antena 3 network, and were later rerun by the same network as well as cable/satellite channels Factoría de Ficción and Paramount Comedy. Antena 3 Internacional satellite channel broadcasts the series to Latin America. The series debuted in 2003 and became popular thanks to its funny characters, witty script, and capacity to integrate and poke fun at contemporary issues; the program presents a caustic satire of many of the 'types' found in Spanish society.

In 2006, Antena 3's rival Telecinco acquired a 15% share of Miramón Mendi, the company that produces the series. Miramón's contract with Antena 3 expired on June 2006 and was not renewed, bringing the series to an end, since the actors' contracts bind them to the production company and not to the network. Miramón Mendi then created a new series for Telecinco with most of the same actors and a similar setting, but with brand-new characters and storyline. *La que se avecina* débuted 22 April 2007.

Characters

Porter's lodge

- **Emilio Delgado Martín** (*Fernando Tejero*) – The building's porter. He is in his mid thirties and lives in the porter's lodge with his father, Mariano. He is an unambitious man who just wants to live without worries and have a steady girlfriend. Unluckily, he is in the wrong building for that. He is a gossip who always has a comeback for everything. He was in college for a while, until he got kicked out. He has had three girlfriends so far: Rocío (a mailman with a young son whom he almost married), Belén (a complicated relationship where they have broken up and gotten together again several times) and Carmen (his college professor). His most well known catchphrase, "un poquito de por favor" (a little bit of please), has quickly become an everyday use idiom around Spain. It has even been parodied in other shows, and not only in the show's own station, Antena 3.

- **Mariano Delgado** (*Eduardo Gómez*) – Emilio's father, though not exactly a model one. He's separated from Emilio's mother and, since he has no place to live, he made himself one with his son. He has a lot of nerve, is a womanizer without much luck, and he's always concocting one money scheme or another. It won't be the first time Emilio has kicked him out, but he always takes him back. His catch phrase is *ignorante de la vida*, criticizing the younger generation for being ignorant about life. He enjoys a brief career as a stand-up comic with his performance being called *Crónicas Marianas*, "The Mariano Chronicles", a reference to the Spanish late-night TV show Crónicas Marcianas. In spite of his unstylish look, he considers himself a metrosexual, much to the amusement of his neighbours and son.

1-A

Radiopatio (roughly translated into "gossip yard") headquarters, as they call their *gossip agency*, home of three old ladies nicknamed *las Supernenas* (The Powerpuff Girls), *las tres mellizas* (The Triplets), and *las brujas de Eastwick* (The Witches of Eastwick) among others. Their common hobbies are gossip, bingo and shoplifting.

- **Vicenta Benito** (*Gemma Cuervo*) – Lives in flat 1-A. She's a retired woman that has never married and who's still a virgin. She's really naive (to the point that she seems dumb) and polite but also very optimistic. Her dog Valentin is the most important thing for her. Alongside her sister Marisa and her friend Concha, they're the source of all gossiping in the building. She's got a crush on Andrés. When Marisa's husband gets back they end up together to everyone's amazement. She is still waiting for her true love. At the first time it seems that she is silly but in fact is very clever when she wants.
- **Maria Luisa "Marisa" Benito** (*Mariví Bilbao*) – Vicenta's older sister. After her husband Manolo left her, Vicenta took her in her home. She's the polar opposite of her sister, a harsh, ironic chain-smoker, "chinchón" (anisette)-drinking who always speaks her mind. She would like to retire to Benidorm with a handsome German. Alongside her sister and her friend Concha, they like to spy on others in the building and spread gossip. Marisa is often seen smoking and carries a large bottle of Chinchón liquor in her purse and wearing teen clothes.
- **Concha** (*Emma Penella*) – In the first season, she lived in flat 2-B with her son Armando and her grandson Dani. Afterwards, they moved out and she sold the flat to the Guerra family. But her son put her in a retirement house because the woman he moved in with didn't like her, which pissed her off. She went to live with her friends Vicenta and Marisa. She still had another flat in the building, which she rented to Belén without a contract. Recently, she decided to sell it, and Belén bought it using a plot that Concha didn't like one bit.

1-B

- **Mauricio "Mauri" Hidalgo** (*Luis Merlo*) – A gay journalist who used to work for a Cosmopolitan-type magazine. He's unstable, hypochondriac, has many obsessions and he's pretty insecure. Mauri frequently finds himself not sure as to whether or not his potential love's interests are gay. During the first season, he lived with his boyfriend Fernando, but he left to work in London. Later he had a son, Ezequiel, by artificial insemination with his lesbian roommate Bea. He also had an affair with Lucia's brother Diego, which ended when Diego got involved with Abel, his baby son's nanny. Fernando has since returned and they're living together again. Recently, Mauri decided to write a book at Fernando's urging and his own lack of fulfillment with his career. After suffering from severe writer's block, he was helped by Mariano to write an action novel featuring a truck driver who is struck by lightning and gains precognition powers. Although he found the story ridiculous, he went with the idea. The book became a best-seller.
- **Fernando Navarro** (*Adrià Collado*) – Mauri's lawyer boyfriend during season 1. After he lost his job when he came out, he got a very good job offer at London and finally decided to take it. They did the long-distance relationship thing for a while, but they finally broke up as friends. He has since returned and, after a bit of fumbling, he and Mauri are living together again. He has decided to start his own practice, and him and Mauri have just married.

2-A

- **Juan Cuesta** (*José Luis Gil*) – A middle-aged high-school teacher and long time strata council president, a position that defines who he is. He's a very grey man, completely controlled by his wife, he's a born worrier and nobody respects him. But, as president of this building, he always sees himself in the middle of some big messy affairs. He's married to Paloma, until she ends up in coma. He then starts an affair with his new neighbour, Isabel and, after a spectacular coming out, they move in together. He has divorced his wife, but has yet married Isabel. He lost his job and his position as strata coulcil president in later seasons, and with them his purpose in life. He has since then found a new job and recovered the strata council presidency.
- **Natalia Cuesta** (*Sofía Nieto*) – Juan and Paloma's teen daughter. She's got a lot more freedom since her mother is in coma. She's had several boyfriends, among them Pablo, with whom she lived under her aunt's roof for a while. She moved out to live on her own, but soon returned and she's now studying psychology. She got pregnant as a surrogate mother for a couple that soon backed out of the deal; she still carries on with her pregnancy. She has started a relationship with Yago.
- **José Miguel "Josemi" Cuesta** (*Eduardo García Martínez*) – Juan and Paloma's son, who is in his early teens. A lazy but gifted boy, always quick to take advantage of

opportunities. José Miguel has the IQ of a genius, and was offered a chance to study abroad in Canada, but opted to stay in Spain. He's in love with Candela, in 2-B.
- **Isabel Ruiz** (*Isabel Ordaz*) – Called *La Hierbas* (herb-woman or "pot head") by her neighbours, she moves in with her family after buying flat 2-B from Concha. A neurotic hypochondriac with a laisser-faire attitude, she's big time into natural therapy, herbal remedies and yoga. After her husband gets jailed, she starts an affair with Juan, which eventually leads to the end of her marriage. She moves in with Juan and his children and eventually sells her flat. After Juan loses his job, she is forced to return to work as a nurse, to her chagrin.
- **Yago** (*Roberto San Martin*) – Nicknamed *el Sabrosón* (the babbler) by the neighbours, is Lucía's Cuban boyfriend, whom she met while on holidays when she was still engaged to Carlos. He's an ecology nut, very active in his NGO *Aldeas Verdes* (Green Villages) and Lucía adopts his principles to get along with him. They've had several crisis when he caught her with Carlos and Roberto. After she leaves for Somalia, he moves into the attic and starts a relationship with Natalia. He now lives with her in the 2-A.

2-B
- **Higinio** (*Ricardo Arroyo*) – used to be building's plumber and building worker until he bought the 2-B flat from Carlos. He's a laid-back man, who doesn't want problems in life. He started reforming 2-A, but then his wife Mamen got angry at them and told him to stop. He now has to work secretly at night.
- **Mamen** (*Emma Ozores*) – Higinio's wife. She likes to have all perfect at home. She is angry with Cuesta family because their son Josemi touched Candela's breast while she was sleeping.
- **Candela** (*Denise Maestre*) – Called *Candy-Candy* by their neighbours. Higinio and Mamen's 14-year-old daughter. She's interested in Pablo, who treats her like a child.
- **Raquel** (*Elena Lombao*) – Mamen's sister, a female-identifying transgender. Her brother in law Higinio insists on calling her Raúl, her birth name. She briefly dated Emilio, but he wasn't able to get over the fact she has male genitalia.
- **Moncho** (*Pablo Chiapella*) – Higinio and Mamen's oldest son, who has just returned home after his business venture collapsed.

3-A
The former home of Lucía, who now has moved to Somalia (see former characters below). It still belongs to her, and her father lived there for a while with his butler and cook while he's having his house refurbished. Natalia and Yago have rented it while the 2-A is undergoing reforms.

3-B
- **Belén López Vázquez** (*Malena Alterio*) – She's nicknamed *la Golfa* (the *Tart*) by her landlady. She rents flat 3-B to Concha, without a contract (a fact she reminds her landlady often). Harsh and fussy, she's very bitter because of her lack of success with men. She doesn't have a steady job and has worked in a lot of occupations (waitress in a burger restaurant and in Lucía's restaurant, receptionist in an undertakers, shop assistant and parking meter controller, among others). She eventually gets together with Emilio, to the point of living together, but they finally break up. Since then, they have broken up and gotten together again several times, including an affair while he was dating Carmen. She had a one night stand with Roberto. She just got a mortgage to buy the flat from Concha. She's now with Paco.
- **Beatriz 'Bea' Villarejo** (*Eva Isanta*) – Mauri's lesbian roommate and best friend. She moved in with Mauri after breaking-up with her girlfriend Inés, when Mauri was looking for a roommate after Fernando left. She's a veterinarian, open, optimistic and sure of herself. She wanted to have a child and asked Mauri to be sperm donor. He wasn't supposed to get involved with raising the child, but finally he did and in a big way. For a while, she dated lesbian lawyer Rosa, but the relationship ended when she made Bea choose between her and Mauri after her son, Ezequiel, was born. After Fernando returned, she moved to 2-B with her new friend Carmen. Now she lives in 3-B with Belén and Ana, her new girlfriend.
- **Ana 'Inga'** (*Vanesa Romero*) – Nicknamed *Inga* or *la Sirenita* (*The Little Mermaid*) by the neighbours, she's a very beautiful, Veela-like air hostess who, after a passionate night with Bea, ends up accepting she's a lesbian and they become a couple. She sporadically works as a model, which makes Bea rather jealous of other men looking at her love interest.
- **Maria Jesús Vázquez** (*Beatriz Carvajal*) – Belen's mother, she's nicknamed *la Torrijas* by the neighbours. She moves in with her when he leaves her husband. She's manipulative and dominant. She has started a relationship with Rafael (see below).

Top floor
- **Pablo Guerra** (*Elio González*) – Isabel and Andrés' youngest son. After his parents' marriage breaks up, he sticks with his father. For a while, he dates and lives with Natalia in Nieves' flat. He moved with his mother after his father left. He dated Marta for a while, but they broke up when she made him choose between her and his friendship with Paco. The two friends now live together on the top floor.
- **Paco** (*Guillermo Ortega*) – The videoshop assistant. A self-proclaimed film lover, Paco has a collection of weird quirks and kinks. He's still a virgin (despite his friends attempts to find a woman to deflower him) because he wants his first time to be with a woman he

loves. He finally finds a girlfriend at Diego and Abel's wedding and he gets very upset when his friends joke about the fact she's not very pretty. They finally get married, but soon thereafter they start having serious problems. Separated from his wife, he has now moved to the top floor apartment with his friend Pablo. He has started relationship with Belen but they split up.

Non-resident characters

- **Rafael Álvarez** (*Nicolás Dueñas*) – Lucías father, who, after his daughter leaves, moved temporaly to her flat with his buttler and cook while he's having his house refurbished. The wealthy owner of a speculative construction company, completely amoral and willing to do anything for money, he tried to buy the building several times, including arsoning it.
- **Marta** (*Assumpta Serna*) – The president of the building on the opposite side of the road. She's nicknamed *pantumaca* due to her strong Catalan accent. Divorced for several years, she falls in love with Juan Cuesta, who hesitates between her and *la hierbas*. After being rejected by Juan she attempts suicide on New Year's Eve but finally accepts it and develops an ambiguous friendship with her rival, since every advice she gives her results in trouble and crisis for the couple. She dated Isabel's youngest son Pablo for a while, until she made him choose between her and his friendship with Paco. She lost.
- **José María** (*Nacho Guerreros*) – A former drug addict, who still has some mental problems due to that, who becomes friends with Emilio and the videoclub gang. He lives with his aunt Choni.
- **Father Miguel** (*Manuel Millán*) – The neighbourhood priest. Ready for everything, he has been able to marry, confess and baptize characters of both sexes and all sexual orientations (as long as they don't tell the bishop). He's a singer (and not a good one) and he's always trying to sell people his singles, usually Catholic covers of hit Spanish songs.

Former characters

- **Paloma Hurtado** (*Loles León*) – Juan's wife for 18 years. A very controlling woman with an acerbic tongue. She ended up in coma after failing down the interior courtyard from her window while fighting with Isabel. She finally got out of her coma, only to be run over with a car by Isabel. She was in coma for a long time, until she died. The day she was cremated Juan discovered that she cheated with a vacuum cleaner seller.

  The reason for Loles León's character death was because the actress asked for a pay rise, since the show was getting good ratings, but the producing company didn't consent, so her character was put into coma until the discussion was solved. While in coma, Paloma appeared a few times on the show, but since Loles wasn't working with them due to the salary problem, her face was never shown, always being facing away or just her legs. When Loles lost her cause with the company and decided to sign off, Paloma's death was produced.
- **Armando** (*Joseba Apaolaza*) – Concha's son. After the first season, he moved away to live in a house with his new girlfriend and tried, unsuccessfully, to put his mother in a retirement home. Fernando being a closeted homosexual, he and Mauri tried to fend off the building suspicions about them being gay by befriending Armando, inviting him over to watch football matches and other considered manly things. Unluckily for them, it was all worthless, since Armando leaves their home (after the match finished) by saying "I thought you gay people were a bit more tactful", after Mauri and Fernando behaved like the stereotypical "macho".
- **Alex Guerra** (*Juan Díaz*) – Isabel and Andrés' oldest son. When the family starts family therapy to try to save the marriage, Isabel confesses Alex is the product of a pre-marriage affair with a Polish man named Jaroslav. When Isabel moves in with Juan, he goes to live with them and gets along very well with his new family. He left the series to find his real father in Poland.
- **Nieves Cuesta** (*Carme Balagué*) – Nicknamed *la Chunga* by the neighbours, she's Juan's single sister. He moved in with him (without asking him first) after Paloma's accident to help him. Unlike her brother, she has a strong character and wants things done her way. She has some money, but she's stingy. She has a fallout with her brother over his relationship with Isabel and, after some trouble, ends up buying Isabel's flat and starting a relationship with her former husband Andrés, trying by all means to get back at her brother. When things between Andrés and her fall through, she moves away, leaving her brother in charge of renting (and later, selling) the flat.
- **Roberto Alonso** (*Daniel Guzmán*) – Lucía's boyfriend. He's an architect, but works drawing erotic comics. He's brilliant, but he has no ambitions and he's lazy. After his relationship with Lucía ends, he moves to the building's attic and tries to get her back several times. After finally giving up, he now lives in 2-B with his ex-rival turned friend Carlos, trying to get him over his depression. He finally moves away to Puerto Banús to continue with his profitable business of drawing caricatures.
- **Carlos** (*Diego Martín*) – Lucía's childhood friend. A rich kid like her, he lives off his family's money. Carlos is very unsure of himself, and ends up doing whacky, impulsive things, such as pretending to be gay and trying to start a relationship with Mauri. He's been after Lucia since forever, but she never wanted anything with him. He helps her with her restaurant business, and gets infatuated with Alicia. Eventually,

he buys the video shop in the ground floor and outs Juan as building president, gaining popular support by paying for a new elevator and spa in the attic. In a new year party, he has a drunken one-night stand with Alba, and she's now pregnant with his daughter, whom he agreed to support. After much trouble, Lucía finally gives him a chance, but it doesn't last long. Totally depressed, he agrees share a flat with Roberto. But he can't get over the depression, and checks himself into a depression clinic, selling both the flat and the videoclub.

- **Lucía Álvarez** (*María Adánez*) – Called *La Pija* (the snooty one). The daughter of the wealthy owner of a construction company, Lucía arrives at the building to live with her boyfriend Roberto. She works in her father's company and she's used to good clothes and the finer things. Eventually, her relationship with Roberto falls through and she decides to quit her father's company and do things by herself. She tries opening a restaurant, but it doesn't work. She goes through some difficult times after she refuses her father's money, but things started to get better once she gave her old boyfriend Carlos another chance. But things fell through quickly. She finds a new boyfriend in Yago, an ecology nut whose principles she adopts to get along with him. In the end, however, she believes in them more than he does and leaves with a NGO to Somalia. As Marisa puts it, her appearance is always neat and stylish, which is emphasized by the catchphrase "qué mona va esta chica siempre" (how well-groomed is always this girl).

- **Andrés Guerra** (*Santiago Ramos*) – Isabel's husband. A middle-aged businessman of doubtful reputation, he has to sell his house after some trouble with the Treasury and he moves with his family to 2-B. He has a sports shop *Deportes Guerra* and he's always into doubtful business affairs. Eventually he's jailed, but he's able to get out when Vicenta pays his bond. But she has a crush on him, and he has to play along so she wouldn't retire the bond money. He suspects his wife is having an affair for a while, but he doesn't know with whom until she tells him in a very inappropriate moment. He later starts a relationship with Nieves which falls through fast. For a while he lives alone in the attic, turning increasingly bitter, with an apparent Diogenes syndrome. He enjoys a brief relationship with Carmen. Finally, after a freak accident, he ends up with amnesia, and Vicenta tries to make him think that they are married. When he realizes that he doesn't have anything left for him at Calle Desengaño 21, he leaves the building and leaves the show for good.

- **Alicia Sanz** (*Laura Pamplona*) – Belen's roommate. A would-be actress, Alicia is vain, selfish, completely without tact and not above rubbing her success with men in her less successful roommate Belen's face. She goes through men like shoes, never falling in love with one. She toys with Carlos for a while, getting pricy gifts from him but never giving him anything in return. Occasionally (very occasionally) a bit of friendly generosity comes through. After Emilio moves up with Belén, they quarrel and Alicia moves in with a now single Lucía. After a while, she and Belén patch things through and she returns to 3-B. Eventually, Alicia finally falls in love with a man, Ricardo, and moves to New York City with him.

- **Carmen Villanueva** (*Llum Barrera*) – A college professor, and the daughter of the vice-chancellor, she meets Emilio when he attends one of her classes and they start a relationship. Carmen knows what she wants and she's very sure of herself, but she has some insane tendencies. After she and Emilio break up, she moves up with Belén to try to recover him, up to the point of calling up her former crazy boyfriend to make him jealous, but it doesn't work. She later rents 2-B from Nieves, and Bea moves with her. She has a crush on Fernando, even after Bea tells her he's gay, and tries to seduce him, but he flees away scared. She lived at 3-B with Bea, Belén and *Inga* for a while, but finally moved back with her parents.

- **Diego Álvarez** (*Mariano Alameda*) – Lucia's younger brother. Recently married to Alba, he meets Mauri at his sister's restaurant opening, and they start an affair. He divorces and moves in with him, but their affair ends when he falls for Abel, the male nanny of Mauri's son Ezequiel. Mauri gets very pissed off and tries to prevent their wedding, but finally he marries Abel, being the first gay married couple in Spain. But soon thereafter, he admits he has made an error, that it was too soon and that he misses Mauri. But Mauri's former boyfriend Fernando (who turns out to be a former college classmate of his) has since then returned.

- **Alba** (*Marta Belenguer*) – Diego's not completely sane wife. Jealous and insecure, she gets the shock of her life when she learns her husband is having an affair with another man. After they divorce, she has a one-night affair with Carlos, and she's now pregnant with his child.

- **Rosa Izquierdo** (*María Almudéver*) – Bea's girlfriend in season 3. A strong-willed lawyer that originally was hired by Bea's former employer against her but that she choose to became her lawyer instead. The two of them soon became a couple, but Rosa and Mauri never got along. In the end, they broke up when Bea choose to go with Mauri to Diego and Abel's wedding (to give him emotional support) instead of going with Rosa to meet her family.

Episodes

1st season

- Episode 1: *Érase una mudanza* (Once upon a moving)
- Episode 2: *Érase una reforma* (Once

- Episode 3: *Érase el reciclaje* (Once upon a recycling)
- Episode 4: *Érase un rumor* (Once upon a rumor)
- Episode 5: *Érase un niño* (Once upon a baby)
- Episode 6: *Érase un resbalón* (Once upon a drop off)
- Episode 7: *Érase una rata* (Once upon a rat)
- Episode 8: *Érase un indigente* (Once upon a beggar)
- Episode 9: *Érase una de miedo* (Once upon a scary movie)
- Episode 10: *Érase un dilema* (Once upon a dilemma)
- Episode 11: *Érase un traspaso* (Once upon a handover)
- Episode 12: *Érase un sustituto* (Once upon a substitute)
- Episode 13: *Érase una fiesta* (Once upon a party)
- Episode 14: *Érase una avería* (Once upon a breakdown)
- Episode 15: *Érase un anillo* (Once upon a ring)
- Episode 16: *Érase una Nochebuena* (Once upon a Christmas Eve)
- Episode 17: *Érase un fin de año* (Once upon a New Year Eve)

2nd season

- Episode 18: *Érase una derrama* (Once upon an apportionment)
- Episode 19: *Érase un sueño erótico* (Once upon an erotic dream)
- Episode 20: *Érase un negocio* (Once upon a business)
- Episode 21: *Érase un desafío* (Once upon a challenge)
- Episode 22: *Érase una patrulla ciudadana* (Once upon a civic patrol)
- Episode 23: *Érase un rastrillo* (Once upon a street market)
- Episode 24: *Érase una huelga* (Once upon a strike)
- Episode 25: *Érase un piso en venta* (Once upon a flat on sale)
- Episode 26: *Érase una parabólica* (Once upon a satellite dish)
- Episode 27: *Érase un video casero* (Once upon a home-made video)
- Episode 28: *Érase unas elecciones* (Once upon an election)
- Episode 29: *Érase una despedida de soltero* (Once upon a stag night)
- Episode 30: *Érase una boda* (Once upon a wedding)
- Episode 31: *Érase un apoyo vecinal* (Once upon a neighborhood support)

3rd season

- Episode 32: *Érase un caos* (Once upon a chaos)
- Episode 33: *Érase un okupa* (Once upon a squatter)
- Episode 34: *Érase un matrimonio de conveniencia* (Once upon a convenience marriage)
- Episode 35: *Érase una inauguración* (Once upon an inauguration)
- Episode 36: *Érase un combate* (Once upon a fight)
- Episode 37: *Érase un canario* (Once upon a canary)
- Episode 38: *Érase un mal de ojo* (Once upon an evil eye)
- Episode 39: *Érase un famoso* (Once upon a celebrity)
- Episode 40: *Érase un desalojo* (Once upon an eviction)
- Episode 41: *Érase un belén* (Once upon a nativity scene)
- Episode 42: *Érase una Nochevieja* (Once upon a New Year's Eve)
- Episode 43: *Érase una grieta* (Once upon a crack)
- Episode 44: *Érase unos nuevos inquilinos* (Once upon new tenants)
- Episode 45: *Érase un bautizo* (Once upon a christening)
- Episode 46: *Érase una academia* (Once upon an academy)
- Episode 47: *Érase unos estatutos* (Once upon some statutes)
- Episode 48: *Érase unas alumnas* (Once upon some female students)
- Episode 49: *Érase un juicio* (Once upon a trial)
- Episode 50: *Érase un disco-pub videoclub* (Once upon a disco-pub videoshop)
- Episode 51: *Érase un cobaya* (Once upon a guinea pig)
- Episode 52: *Érase un premio* (Once upon a prize)
- Episode 53: *Érase unas puertas blindadas* (Once upon some security doors)
- Episode 54: *Érase un vicio* (Once upon a vice)
- Episode 55: *Érase un administrador* (Once upon an administrator)
- Episode 56: *Érase un traición* (Once upon a treason)
- Episode 57: *Érase el primer presidente gay* (Once upon the first gay president)
- Episode 58: *Érase una tragaperras* (Once upon a slot machine)
- Episode 59: *Érase un desgobierno* (Once upon a misgovern)
- Episode 60: *Érase un regalo de boda* (Once upon a wedding present)
- Episode 61: *Érase otra boda* (Once upon another wedding)
- Episode 62: *Érase una luna de miel* (Once upon a honeymoon)
- Episode 63: *Érase un cirujano plástico* (Once upon a plastic surgeon)
- Episode 64: *Érase unas vacaciones* (Once upon some holidays)

4th season

- Episode 65: *Érase un despertar* (Once upon a wakeup)
- Episode 66: *Érase un cultivo* (Once upon a crop)
- Episode 67: *Érase un desvío provisional* (Once upon a provisional detour)
- Episode 68: *Érase una sequía* (Once upon a drought)
- Episode 69: *Érase un banco en la acera* (Once upon a bench in the sidewalk)
- Episode 70: *Érase una Navidad convulsa* (Once upon a convulsed Christmas)
- Episode 71: *Érase la tercera Nochevieja* (Once upon the third New Year's Eve)
- Episode 72: *Érase unos propósitos de Año Nuevo* (Once upon some New Year resolutions)
- Episode 73: *Érase una presidenta títere* (Once upon a puppet president)
- Episode 74: *Érase un par de bodas* (Once upon a pair of weddings)
- Episode 75: *Érase una conexión Wifi* (Once upon a Wifi connection)
- Episode 76: *Érase un vudú* (Once upon a voodoo)
- Episode 77: *Érase un día de San Valentín* (Once upon a Saint Valentine's Day)

- Episode 78: *Érase una nueva vida* (Once upon a new life)

5th season
- Episode 79: *Érase una extradición* (Once upon an extradition)
- Episode 80: *Érase un colapso* (Once upon a collapse)
- Episode 81: *Érase un robot de cocina* (Once upon a kitchen robot)
- Episode 82: *Érase un presidente de vacaciones* (Once upon a president on holidays)
- Episode 83: *Érase un anuncio* (Once upon an advertisement)
- Episode 84: *Érase un billete de 50 euros* (Once upon a 50 euro bill)
- Episode 85: *Érase un escándalo* (Once upon a scandal)
- Episode 86: *Érase un descubrimiento macabro* (Once upon a macabre discovery)
- Episode 87: *Érase una emisora pirata* (Once upon a pirate radio)
- Episode 88: *Érase un funeral con sorpresa* (Once upon a funeral with surprise)
- Episode 89: *Érase una lista de boda* (Once upon a bridal registry)
- Episode 90: *Érase un paripé* (Once upon an act)
- Episode 91: *Érase un adios* (Once upon a good-bye)

Catchphrases

Porter
- **Emilio**
  - *¡Un poquito de por favor!* (A little bit of please!)
  - *¡Cipote!* (Cock!)
  - *Apaguen los teléfonos móviles y no fumen, para hablar levantan la mano y para insultar también me la levantan* (Please turn off your mobile telephones and do not smoke. To speak, raise your hand and to insult, raise your hand too.)
  - *¡Papá, comete el kiwi!* (Dad, eat your kiwi!)
- **Mariano**
  - *Tú... ignorante de la vida* (You... know nothing about life.")
  - *Mariano Delgado, metrosexual y pensador* (Mariano Delgado, metrosexual and thinker)

1-A
- **Vicenta**
  - *A Marisa le dejó Manolo* (Marisa was dumped by Manolo)
- **Marisa**
  - *¡Qué mona va esta chica siempre!* (This girl always looks so cute! – referring to Lucía)
  - *¡Radio Patio, 24 horas!* (Radio Patio, 24 hours!)
  - *¡Movida!* (Action!)
  - *¡Y a éste qué le importa lo que hizo Manolo!* (What Manolo did is none of his business!)
  - *¡¿Por qué siempre me tienes que meter a Manolo en todas partes?!* (Why do you always have to mention Manolo?!)
- **Concha**
  - *Váyase Señor Cuesta... ¡Váyase!* (Leave Mr. Cuesta—Leave now! – paraphrasing a famous phrase former Prime Minister José María Aznar said to then Prime Minister Felipe González)
  - *¡Chorizo!* (You thief!)
  - *¡Qué vergüenza! (How shameful!)*

1-B
- **Mauri**
  - *¡Envidia de pene!* (Penis envy! – especially to Rosa)
  - *Este también es gay* (This one is gay too.)

2-A
- **Juan**
  - *¡Qué follón!* (What a bloody mess!)
  - *Soy Juan Cuesta, presidente de esta nuestra comunidad* (I'm Juan Cuesta, Strata Council President)
- **Paloma**
  - *¡Aquí no, Juan, aquí no!* (Not here, Juan, not here!)
  - *¡Hombre ya!* (No way!)
  - *¡Y punto en Boca, Y punto en Boca!* (And that's it. period!)

In other countries

Portugal – Aqui não há quem viva
The series has the same setting and plots, though the names of most of characters change, with Portuguese actors.

France – Faites comme chez vous
The script is the same but the actors and the building changes.

Serbia – Moje drage komšije
On Studio B from April 29, 2011. Translated *Moje drage komšije* (English: *My Beloved Neighbors*). The show replaces Los Hombres de Paco. It was previously aired in its entirety on the B92 network.

Bosnia and Herzegovina – Moje drage komšije
NTV Hayat

Greece – Η Πολυκατοικία
Premiering on Mega Channel on 6 October 2008.Now it's in second season.

Mexico – Vecinos
The series portrays the same kind of characters, living all together in those buildings. Different names and actors.

Italy – Qui non si può vivere
Same setting and presumably same characters. There aren't updated news on this subject, only that the first season will be composed by 26 episodes of 50 minutes each. It should be filmed very soon.

Argentina – Aquí no hay quien viva
The script is similar but the actors and the building changes. However, it didn't had a lot of succes as it had in Spain and also because of the schedule problems that Telefé was having and ended up.

Colombia – Aquí no hay quien viva
The script, the setting and the plots are the same with some little changes though the names of most of characters

change, with Colombian actors. RCN bought the rights to make a local adaptation, which began airing on August 25, 2008 but ended on February 27, 2009 despite the success that was having.

Finland – Naapureina Madridissa

On YLE TV1. Translated *Naapureina Madridissa* (As Neighbours in Madrid). The broadcasting of the show started on May 25, 2010.

Bulgaria - Щурите съседи

Щурите съседи - from Bulgarian "The Crazy Neighbours". The broadcasting of the show started for second time on December 29, 2010.

United States - I hate this place

American television network ABC announced that it's going to produce an American version of the series, that will be named *I hate this place*. Craig Doyle will be responsible for the first scripts of the series, and it will be directed by Ben Silverman and Sofía Vergara. Filming will start in early 2011.

Awards

- Fotogramas de Plata: Best Actor (Fernando Tejero) (2005), Best Actress (Loles León) (2004)
- ATV Award: Best Actor (Luis Merlo, 2005), Best Actress (Malena Alterio, 2005), Best Screenplay (2005), Best Fiction Program (2005).
- TP de Oro: Best National Series (2005), Best Actor (Fernando Tejero, 2005).
- Ondas Award: Best Series (2004), tied with *Los Serrano*.

Source (edited): "http://en.wikipedia.org/wiki/Aqu%C3%AD_no_hay_quien_viva"

Aída

Aída is a Spanish comedy sitcom set in Madrid, that spun off from another sitcom called *7 Vidas*. The show first aired on January 16, 2005 and is produced by Globomedia for the Spanish network Telecinco. It currently started its sixth season.

The show stars Carmen Machi as the title character, Aída García, a working, single mom with two teenage children, forced to move with her mother and brother to make ends meet.

The show has received favorable criticism from the audience and has been the most viewed show in Spain since 2007. It has also received several awards like the Ondas Award for Best Spanish Sitcom.

Plot

The show follows the life of Aída García (Carmen Machi) who has to move to a somewhat seedy neighbourhood with her mother, Eugenia (Marisol Ayuso), and brother, Luisma (Paco León). Together with Aída, come her two teenage children, Jonathan and Lorena (David Castillo and Ana María Polvorosa).

Other than her family, Aída spends time with her best friend/prostitute, Paz (Melanie Olivares); Chema, a smart store-owner (Pepe Viyuela), and his effeminate son, Fidel (Eduardo Casanova); and Mauricio, a chauvinist bar-owner (Mariano Peña).

Life without Aida

Changes were made in Season 6. Aída has been written out of the series (the character is now supposed to be in prison), as Carmen Machi has left the show to pursue new projects. Soraya and her daughter Aida Jr. have been introduced. Mauricio has changed and toned down his chauvinistic rhetoric and fallen for Soraya. Jonathan has been made "dumber" as a result of going through puberty. Wenceslao has been given more presence.

Location

The show is located in a fictional neighbourhood called Esperanza Sur. However, it can be inferred that it is located in the district of Carabanchel, in the south part of Madrid. This can be demonstrated by the inclusion of the Urgel subway entrance, which is located in Carabanchel, as well as from the appearance of the 2-3 story buildings with green windows, common sights in that district.

Characters

García García Family

- **Aída García García** (Carmen Machi) - A 45 year old, divorced woman. She's short, with a high-pitched voice. She has three children and works mostly as a cleaning lady. She got pregnant of her first daughter, Soraya, when she was 17, so she eloped with her fiance, Manolo. However, they got divorced several years later when she found out he spent the money in prostitutes. Before divorcing, they had their other two children: Lorena and Jonathan. Aída lives with her mother, Eugenia, and her brother Luis Mariano, best known as Luisma, and her two younger children (Soraya moved when she turned 18). Aída usually has several jobs to make ends meet. She wanted to finish her studies, but couldn't. She is an alcoholic, although she no longer drinks.
- **Luis Mariano "Luisma" García García** (Paco León) - A 35 year old, ex-junkie, rehabilitated after going through *Proyecto Hombre*. He has a good heart, but is somewhat dimwitted. He is Aída's younger brother, and Eugenia's son. Ever since he was 13, he has tried to have sex with Paz, his childhood friend.

Luisma (Paco León) and Aída (Carmen Machi), main characters of Aída

- **Eugenia García** (Marisol Ayuso) - A 65 year old overweight widow. She is the mother of Aída and Luisma. When her husband died, she had to accept her daughter and grandchildren moving to her house. Eugenia thinks she's famous because she used to sing at a club. She was known by the name "La Bim Bam Bum".
- **Soraya García García** (Miren Ibarguren) - Aída's oldest daughter. She moved out of her home when she turned 18 due to her mother's constant alcoholism. She joined the cast in the sixth season. She returned home with her only daughter, Aída Jr., fleeing from her abusive husband. He comes to "Esperanza Sur" looking for her and finds her with Aida, who accidentally kills him with an iron, trying to defend her daughter from his abuses.
- **Lorena García García** (Ana María Polvorosa) - Aída's 20 year old, second daughter. She is known for her red hair and her endless string of boyfriends. She enjoys playing pranks on Luisma and Eugenia, along with her brother Jonathan.
- **Jonathan García García** (David Castillo) - Aída's 16 year old, youngest child. Far from being an ideal son, Jonathan has long hair, wears an earring, is disrespectful, steals, and has had several run-ins with the law. However, he still remains noble at heart.

The Neighbours

- **José María "Chema" Martínez** (Pepe Viyuela) - A 45 year old bald, divorced man. He is the owner of the market store "La Colonial". Chema is an intelligent, educated man, but although he has a degree in Hispanic philology, he hasn't been able to find an according job. This makes him - at times - the butt of jokes in the neighbourhood. He has been friend of Aída and Luisma since childhood. When he was 18, he was Aída's date to their prom. He has a 16 year old son called Fidel, but he's divorced since his ex-wife cheated on him.
- **Fidel Martínez** (Eduardo Casanova) - Chema's 16 year old son. He is somewhat of an outcast in the neighbourhood for his intelligence, his knowledge about almost anything, his hobbies (dancing and painting), and for being very effeminate. He has few friends, but Jonathan is one of them. He is openly gay.
- **Paz Bermejo** (Melanie Olivares) - Aída's 34 year old best friend. They've known each other since childhood. She is a sweet and good woman, despite working as a prostitute for 10 years for lack of a better job. She dislikes her job and keeps it mostly secret, and only her close friends (Aída, Chema, Luisma, and Fidel) know about it. She pretends to be a nurse in front of Aída's children, and a flight attendant to the neighbourhood.
- **Mauricio Colmenero** (Mariano Peña) - A 50 year old man. Bearer of some of the most unwanted traits in a man: chauvinist, fascist, exploiter, perverted, xenophobe, and homophobe. He is a bullfight aficionado and a fan of Burt Reynolds. That's why he named his bar after him (Bar Reinols) and has several pictures of the actor in a wall. He enjoys making fun of other people, especially Chema. He is also noted for treating disrepecfully one of his employees, Oswaldo Wenceslao, whom he calls "Macchu Picchu".

Awards

Ondas Awards
- 2008 - Best Female Actress (Carmen Machi)
- 2006 - Best National Show

ATV Awards
- 2007 - Best Actress (Carmen Machi)
- 2007 - Best Actor (Paco León)
- 2007 - Best Script
- 2005 - Best Actor (Paco León)

TP de Oro
- 2007 - Best Actress (Carmen Machi)
- 2005 - Best Actress (Carmen Machi)
- 2005 - Best Actor (Paco León)

Fotogramas de Plata
- 2007 - Best TV Actress (Carmen Machi)
- 2007 - Best TV Actor (Paco León)
- 2005 - Best TV Actress (Carmen Machi)
- 2005 - Best TV Actor (Paco León)

Screen Actors Guild Awards
- 2006 - Best Supporting TV Actor (Mariano Peña)
- 2005 - Best Lead TV Actress (Carmen Machi)
- 2005 - Best Lead TV Actor (Paco León)
- 2005 - Best Supporting TV Actor (Pepe Viyuela)

Episodes

Broadcasters
- Spain - Telecinco
- Mexico - TV Azteca
- Puerto Rico - CaribeVisión
- Bulgaria - bTV Comedy

Source (edited): "http://en.wikipedia.org/wiki/A%C3%ADda"

El Hormiguero

El Hormiguero (Spanish for "**The Anthill**") is a Spanish television program with a live audience focusing on comedy, science, and politics running since September 2006. It is hosted and produced by screenwriter Pablo Motos and airs on Cuatro, a Spanish television station. Recurring guests on the show include Luis Piedrahita, Raquel Martos, Flipi (the scientist), and puppet ants Trancas and Barrancas (names taken from the Spanish expression "a Trancas y Barrancas" what means "in fits and starts"). It has proved a ratings success, and has expanded from a weekly 120-minute show to a daily 40-minute show in its third season, which began on September 17, 2007. The show won the Entertainment prize at the 2009 Rose d'Or ceremony.

Format

The show is based on an earlier radio program, broadcasted on M80 Radio, called *No Somos Nadie* ("We Are Nobody"). This show continued until June 2007, when Pablo Motos announced that he would be leaving the program to allow the daily production of *El Hormiguero*. *No Somos Nadie* returned in September 2007 with new on-air talent, since most of the old show's talent were part of the television show.

Barrancas (left) and *Trancas* (right) sing along with the show's rap

Segments on the show include science experiments with Flipi, which have included a car running on vegetable oil, hangover cures, a superconductivity demonstration, and various chemical reaction demonstrations. Each episode features a satirical rap, commentary on current events, and humorous phrases as spoken by children. Other segments include pitches for viewers to plant trees and "El Kiosco," a section of magazine reviews. The show also airs parodies of other media, which have included *Back to the Future*, *Pop Idol*, *House*, and *Mission: Impossible*. Many episodes have featured special celebrity guests, including Boris Izaguirre, David Bisbal, Alejandro Sanz, Paulina Rubio, and numerous international celebrities such as Miley Cyrus, Ashley Tisdale or Hugh Jackman. Special guests on the show are sometimes involved throughout the episode, including taking part in the various stunts and science experiments. A number of changes to the show, including new segments such as a webcam call-in portion from viewers, were planned for the upcoming format change in the third season, however this segment and some others like training of wild monkeys were removed, the first one due to the amount of time needed and the second one due to low popularity among the audience.

A very popular segment that was later introduced is Extreme Survival, that features "El maestro empanao" (which roughly translates as "Master Dumbass") Marron and the host Pablo Motos testing out tips and hints on how to survive extreme situations or conditions (such as how to survive being overrun by a car, trapped in a falling lift, attacked by a pack of wolves, etc.). Another popular segment includes *Trancas* and *Barrancas* making fun of the day's news. A satirical news show in which puppets read the news, Las noticias del guiñol, formerly aired on Cuatro.

International attention

The show first received international attention in 2006 for having people walk across a swimming pool filled with a non-Newtonian fluid, a suspension of cornstarch and water called oobleck, that was mixed in a cement truck. This experiment was performed in an October 2006 episode of the show and was repeated with a new batch of oobleck on the Christmas Eve special episode due to its popularity. In 2007, Cuatro signed an agreement with YouTube that allows clips from Cuatro programs, including *El Hormiguero*, to be showcased on the site. In 2009, El Hormiguero was awarded as the best entertainment program in the international Rose d'Or awards. The win was the fourth time a Spanish program has received the award, the first since 1994.

Since 2008, the show has received a large number of appearances from international celebrities including professional wrestlers Batista and Rey Mysterio from WWE, the actors Hugh Jackman, Adam Sandler, Matt Dallas, Sylvester Stallone; Lost stars Matthew Fox and Jorge Garcia; Tokio Hotel; The Jonas Brothers, The Backstreet Boys, Will Smith, Kylie Minogue, Jaden Smith, Jada Pinkett Smith, Jackie Chan, Hugh Grant, Rob Schneider, Michael C. Hall, Jean Reno, Ashley Tisdale, the young actresses Selena Gomez, Miley Cyrus, Justin Timberlake, and comedian Sacha Baron Cohen.

In 2009, Siete y Acción licensed the show's format to an Italian production company to produce a local version of the show. Also in 2009, a Chilean and a Brazilian versions were produced only to meet bad reviews in both countries.

After Jesse Eisenberg spoke negatively about his bad experience on the show, El Hormiguero, in an interview with Conan O'Brien on TBS's Conan, Pablo Motos gave a humorous answer to the actor and the talk-show host from the Spanish program.

Cast

- Pablo Motos - Himself - Host
- Juan Ibáñez Pérez - Himself - *Trancas*
- Damián Molla Herman - Himself - *Barrancas*
- Enrique Pérez Vergara ("Flipy") - El Científico Loco(The Mad Scientist)(Until 5th season)
- Jandro - El Experto en Todo(The Expert in Everything) and Contador de chistes con carteles (Jokes with posters)(5th season)
- Raquel Martos González - Herself
- Luis Piedrahita - *El Rey de las Cosas Pequeñas* (The King of Little Things) and "Mago que revela sus propios trucos" (Wizard that reveals his own stunts)(5th season)
- Jorge Marrón Martín - *El Maestro Empanao* (The Dumbass Master), "El efecto mariposa" (The Butterfly effect), "El cientifico" (5th Season, The Scientist)

Source (edited): "http://en.wikipedia.

El Intermedio

El Intermedio is a satirical news program hosted by Spanish comedian El Gran Wyoming. It is aired in access prime-time, from 9.30pm, on Spain sixth nationwide channel laSexta.

The writers are Alberto López, Alberto González Vázquez, Lola Zambade, Eva Nuño Gómez, Nuria Dominguez, Diego Solanas, Eduardo García Eyo, Sergio Sarria Ruiz, Juan José López and Miguel Ángel Hernández. Alberto González Vázquez is also the author of the popular segment *videos manipulados* (counterfeit videos).
Source (edited): "http://en.wikipedia.org/wiki/El_Intermedio"

El día después

El día depués (English: *The day after*) is a Spanish football show shown on Canal+. It is hosted by former Valencia goalkeeper Santiago Cañizares and the journalist Juanma Castaño.

Presenters
- Ignacio Lewin (1990—1994)
- Michael Robinson (1991—2005)
- Francisco José Carrasco (1994—1997)
- Josep Pedrerol (1997—2004)
- Santiago Cañizares (2009—)
- Juan Manuel Castaño (2009—)

Source (edited): "http://en.wikipedia.org/wiki/El_d%C3%ADa_despu%C3%A9s"

Escenas de Matrimonio

Escenas de Matrimonio TV is a series issued by the Spanish television network, Telecinco, produced by Alba Adriatica (Branch producer Miramon Mendi), premiered on August 1, 2007 showing the reactions of fun couples who live in the same building situations Similar deals in their daily lives.

Matrimoniadas

La Primera de TVE (2002-2004)

The idea of the show comes in 2002 as a separate program sketches varieties Spanish Television,*Noche de Fiesta*, led by José Luis Moreno. His nephews Alberto and Laura Caballero are responsible for the direction and screenplay respectively in this mini-comedy, which soon becomes one of the most celebrated of the program.

In this first actors who gave life to the characters Marisa Porcel (Pepa), Pepe Ruiz (Avelino) Silvia Gambino (Marina) and Alfredo Cernuda (Roberto). The characters of the young couple, less defined, did not even have names at this stage and were interpreted by Manuel Belmonte and Ruth Arteaga. In the next season would be replaced by Rosana Manso and Javier Coromina, and sometimes Martin Czehmester.

Antena 3 (2004)

Once terminated the program in June 2004, some of his players joined, playing the same characters in the series of Antena 3*La sopa boba*, boba is issued until the end of 2004. The roles were played by Marisa Porcel (Pepa), Pepe Ruiz (Avelino) Silvia Gambino (Marina) and Alfredo Cernuda (Roberto). At this stage there is a young couple.

Theater (2003-2006)

Given the great success of the idea, the sketch takes the stage, and between 2003 and 2006 tours are conducted throughout Spain, under the title*Matrimoniadas: Until death do us part*. In 2005 and 2006, the role of Roberto's going to be interpreted by Santiago Urrialde and the young couple is played by Paloma Figueroa and Mario Barbero following Pepe Ruiz, Marisa Porcel and Silvia Gambino in the papers Avelino, Pepa and Marina respectively.

Finally the role premieres in Teatro La Latina in Madrid, and represents April and November 2005 with the following list: Marisa Porcel Pepe Ruiz, Silvia Gambino, Alfredo Cernuda, Rosana Manso and Martin Czehmester.

Telecinco: Escenas de Matrimonio (2007-)

So it all started

Since August 1, 2007, restores the original idea, issued daily in the chain Telecinco Series *Escenas de Matrimonio*, with great success for a hearing on the same pattern of independent and sketches in which, as a novelty, have joined David Venancio Muro in the role of Roberto, Soledad Mallol in the Marina as a middle-aged couple; Miren Ibarguren at Sonia and Daniel Muriel in the role of Miguel, and young couples. Pepe Ruiz and repeated Avelino as Marisa Porcel and Pepa respectively being the older partner.

Besides the main characters in the series can also be seen as secondary Ramon (Ruben Sanz)the attractive best friend Miguel (Daniel Muriel), which Sonia (Miren Ibarguren) does not support, Berta (Marta Poveda), the best friend Sonia (Miren Ibarguren), a married with children who are lees to every man who is, who is also bundled with Ramon (Ruben Sanz), Paco (Jesus Caba), the doorman of the building where they live to make any marriage because of a tip or Desislava (Emilia Uutinen), the beautiful assistant of Pepa (Marisa Porcel) and Avelino (Pepe Ruiz).

He also noted epsisódicos characters like Laura (Rosa Clara Garcia), the best friend Marina (Soledad Mallol), married with one child to give her friend advice on marriage, Cayetana (Carmen Esteban), Pepa's best friend (Marisa Porcel), who loves to meddle with his friend and Domingo (Ibon Uzkudun), the former Sonia (Miren Ibarguren) not to stop the can to the young couple.

Abandonment of Pepa and Avelino and incorporation of Paca and Natalio

At the end of 2007 Pepe Ruiz (Avelino) and Marisa Porcel (Pepa) left *Escenas de Matrimonio* in full success, following sign for Antena 3. Joined them immediately to Antena 3 where the two are currently working in La Familia Mata.

In early 2007 was incorporated as a substitute for another marriage Pepa (Marisa Porcel) and Avelino (Pepe Ruiz), performed by Manuel Galiana and Mary Carmen Ramirez as Natalio and Paca respectively.

Desislava (Emilia Uutinen), the assistant Pepa (Marisa Porcel) and Avelino (Pepe Ruiz), followed in the series despite the abandonment of these, playing the same role and being now assistant Paca (Mary Carmen Ramirez) and Natalio (Manuel Galiana).

Cayetana (Carmen Esteban), the best friend of Pepa (Marisa Porcel), also remains in the series now best friend Paca (Mary Carmen Ramirez) after abandoning Pepa (Marisa Porcel) and Avelino (Pepe Ruiz).

New marriage, Cesareo and Brígida

At the end of February 2008, he joined another marriage, performed by Cesareo Estebanez that plays Cesareo and Mamen Garcia who plays Brigida, the retired guys playing Paco (Jesus Caba), adding to the series most decorated, as the portal or the house of Paco (Jesus Caba), where they are coupled.

In the new season, Brigida (Mamen Garcia) and Cesareo (Cesareo Estebanez) have changed after touching decorated the lottery and buy another apartment in the building. Both hire Desislava (Emilia Uutinen) as an assistant after abandoning Paca (Mary Carmen Ramirez) and Natalio (Manuel Galiana).

Also Sigur (Martin Czehmesther), the boyfriend Desislava (Emilia Uutinen) to be mad at all women in the building.

In the new season following the abandonment of Paca (Mary Carmen Ramirez) and Natalio (Manuel Galiana), Cayetana (Carmen Esteban), the best friend of Pepa (Marisa Porcel) and then Paca (Mary Carmen Ramirez), will become the best friend Brigida (Mamen Garcia) where they share many scenes with her.

New partner, Ricardo and Eufemia, which could already see in the series

In July 2008, began broadcasting scenes of Eufemia (Marta Puig) and Ricardo (Juan Jesus Valverde), Miguel's mother (Daniel Muriel) and Sonia's father (Miren Ibarguren), respectively, which could already be seen in the series, but with Miguel (Daniel Muriel) and Sonia (Miren Ibarguren).

But it was only at the end of the first season since beginning the second season, as before leaving again, sharing some scenes with Miguel (Daniel Muriel) Ainhoa and (Mar Saura). Although occasionally leave them with two scenes alone.

Abandonment Natalio and Paca

Mary Carmen Ramirez (Paca) and Manuel Galiana (Natalio) have abandoned the series because it split up and the floor where they lived, but Emilia Uutinen (Desislava), assistance Paca (Mary Carmen Ramirez) and Natalio (Manuel Galiana) is still in the series despite the abandonment of these, now as assistant Brigida (Mamen Garcia) and Cesareo (Cesareo Estebanez) after moving to another floor.

It also incorporates Martin Czehmester as Sigur, the boyfriend Desislava (Emilia Uutinen), of which he saw in some chapters of the first season, but now sharing scenes with Brigida (Mamen Garcia) and Cesareo (Cesareo Estebanez).

Cayetana (Carmen Esteban), the best friend of Paca (Mary Carmen Ramirez), will become the best friend Brigida (Mamen Garcia) following the abandonment of Paca (Mary Carmen Ramirez) and Natalio (Manuel Galiana).

Abandonment and Ramon Sonia and incorporating Ainhoa

Miren Ibarguren (Sonia) following sign for Aída leaves the series, which will leave your kid by Ramon (Rubén Sanz) is also up in the series.

Replacing Sonia (Miren Ibarguren) has been Ainhoa (Mar Saura) a divorced lawyer who will be the new partner Miguel (Daniel Muriel). Although initially only companions were flat gradually love.

Also in place of Ramon (Rubén Sanz) has joined Nico (Antonio Moreno), Ramon's cousin (Rubén Sanz), now is the best Miguel Friend (Daniel Muriel), but with a smaller role than that of Ramon (Rubén Sanz).

Domingo (Ibon Uzkudun), the former Sonia (Miren Ibarguren) also disappears from the series by abandoning it.

Incorporating Asun and Emilio

Also includes a new marriage, Silvia Gambino and Santiago Urrialde as Asun and Emilio, a middle-aged marriage that are not supported each other.

Her mother, Florinda, played by Lina Morgan will be very top of them, being anxious to get divorced because they do not support Emilio (Santiago Urrialde). At three weeks of its introduction, Lina Morgan (Florinda) left the series for health reasons.

Weeks later he announced the incorporation of Empar Ferrer as Lupe, the millionaire aunt Asun (Silvia Gambino), which also supports Emilio (Santiago Urrialde).

Characters

Actors

- **Ainhoa** (Mar Saura)
- **Miguel** (Daniel Muriel)
- **Roberto** (David Venancio Muro)
- **Marina** (Soledad Mallol)
- **Emilio** (Santiago Urrialde)
- **Asun** (Silvia Gambino)
- **Berta** (Marta Poveda)

- **Sigur** (Martin Czehmester)
- **Brigida** (Mamen Garcia)
- **Cesareo** (Cesareo Estebanez)
- **Desislava** (Emilia Uutinen)
- **Paco** (Jesus Caba)

Minor
- **Eufemia** (Marta Puig)
- **Ricardo** (Juan Jesus Valverde)

Episodic characters
- **Nico** (Antonio Moreno)
- **Lupe** (Empar Ferrer)
- **Laura** (Rosa Clara Garcia)
- **Cayetana** (Carmen Esteban)

Past characters
- **Sonia** (Miren Ibarguren)
- **Avelino** (Pepe Ruiz)

- **Pepa** (Marisa Porcel)
- **Natalio** (Manuel Galiana)
- **Paca** (Mary Carmen Ramirez)
- **Ramon** (Ruben Sanz)
- **Florinda** (Lina Morgan)
- **Domingo** (Ibon Uzkudun)

Source (edited): "http://en.wikipedia.org/wiki/Escenas_de_Matrimonio"

Física o Química

Física o Química (English: *Physics or Chemistry* or *Physical or Chemical*) is a Spanish television series that is an original broadcast of Antena 3. The first episode premiered on 4 February 2008.

Before its official release, *Física o Química* was released on cell phones in *Vodafone live!* and on the official website of Antena 3. After the success of the first season, which ended on 31 March 2008, Antena 3 announced the filming of a new season which would feature more episodes and few cast changes. The second season premiered on 4 September 2008, with guest appearances by Michel Brown and María Casal, among others; it ended on 8 December 2008. The third season premiered on 13 April 2009 and included new characters portrayed by Óscar Sinela, Sandra Blázquez, Miriam Giovanelli, Adrián Rodríguez, Irene Sánchez and José Manuel Seda, and the entry of character actor Álex Barahona who had already appeared on the show, thus compensating for the departure of Michel Brown, Andrés Cheung, Karim El-Kerem and Xavi Mira. Antena 3 confirmed the filming of the fourth season with Adrián Rodríguez as a regular character and the return of Leonor Martín.

Season 6 premiered September 15th on Antena 3. FoQ has been renewed for a seventh season with the departure of Nuria González, Úrsula Corberó, Angy Fernandez and Jose Manuel Seda. The season will be filming in February 28 2011.

Cast and characters

Zurbarán School staff
- Ana Milán as Olimpia Díaz, English language teacher and former principal.
- Marc Clotet as Vicente Vaquero, Gymnastic teacher (Season 4 — present)
- Olivia Molina as Verónica Lebrón, Language and literature teacher and the mother of Teresa (Season 5 — present)
- Cristina Alcázar as Marina Conde, Philosophy teacher (Season 5 — present)
- Sergio Mur as Jorge, Arts teacher and former school counselor (Season 6 — Season 7; recurring Season 5)
- Enrique Arce as Arturo Ochando, Biology teacher (Season 7 — present; recurring Season 6)

Students
- Andrea Duro as Yolanda "Yoli" Freire Caballar
- Javier Calvo as Fernando "Fer" Redondo
- Sandra Blázquez as Alma Núñez (Season 3 — present)
- Adrián Rodríguez as David Ferrán (Season 4 — present; recurring Season 3)
- Lucía Ramos as Teresa Parra (Season 5 — present)
- Álex Batllori as Álvaro (Season 5 — present)
- Nasser Saleh as Rashid "Román" Lorente (Season 5 — present)
- Lorena Mateo as Daniela Vaquero (Season 6 — present; recurring Season 5)
- Alex Hernández as Jon (Season 6 — present)
- Alex Martínez as Salvador "Salva" Quintanilla (Season 6 — present)

Recurring characters
- Isaak Ferriz as Luís Parra, Teresa's father (Season 5 — present)
- Israel Rodríguez as Borja, Fer's boyfriend (Season 6 — present)
- Farah Hamed as Fátima, Rashid's mother (Season 6 — present)

Past characters
- Michel Gurfi as Jonathan, former physical education teacher and love interest of Blanca. Leaves Zurbarán to return to Mexico. (Season 1)
- Fele Martínez as Mario Barrio, the former boyfriend of Irene. He leaves after realizing she is sleeping with Isaac. (Season 1; special guest star Season 2)
- Karim El-Kerem as Isaac Blasco, Zurbarán student and ex-lover of Irene. Dies due to injuries suffered in a quad accident. (Season 1 — Season 2)
- Andrés Cheung as Jan Taeming, Zurbarán student. Returns to China after entering an arranged marriage to his cousin. (Season 1 — Season 2)
- Xavi Mira as Félix, music and drawing teacher. Leaves Colegio Zurbarán after his wife Olympia ultimately chooses Roque over him. (Season 1 — Season 2; special guest star Season 3 and Season 5)
- Michel Brown as Miguel Belaza, the Argentine history and drama teacher (Season 2)
- Leonor Martín as Covandonga "Cova" Ariste, Zurbarán student and girlfriend of Julio (Season 1 — Season 3, special guest star Season 5 and Season 6)
- Joaquín Climent as Adolfo Madroña Bermudez — Director of Studies

- and father of Roque. (Season 1 — Season 4)
- Irene Sánchez as Violeta Calvo, Zurbarán student (Season 3 — Season 4)
- Cecilia Freire as Blanca Román, Language and literature teacher and best friend and roommate of Irene. (Season 1 — Season 4)
- Óscar Sinela as Joaquín "Quino", Zurbarán student (Season 3 — Season 4)
- Blanca Romero as Irene Calvo, Zurbarán's Philosophy professor (Season 1 — Season 4)
- Bart Santana as Roque Madroña Castro, Art teacher (Season 1 — Season 5)
- Adam Jezierski as Gorka Martínez (Season 1 — Season 5, special guest star Season 5 and Season 6)
- Maxi Iglesias as César Cabano de Vera (Season 1 — Season 5)
- Gonzalo Ramos as Julio de la Torre (Season 1 — Season 6)
- Álex Barahona as Berto Freire Caballar, Cafeteria Waiter and the brother of Yoli (Season 3 — Season 6; recurring Season 2)
- Nuria González as Clara Yáñez, English language teacher and former principal. (Season 1 — Season 6)
- José Manuel Seda as Martín Aguilar, school counselor and principal (Season 3 — Season 6)
- Angy Fernández as Paula Blasco (Season 1 — Season 6)
- Úrsula Corberó as Ruth Gómez (Season 1 — Season 6)

Past recurring characters
- Julio Soler as Rubén de la Torre, Julio's brother who kills himself in the pilot (Season 1)
- Nancy Yao as Xiao Mei, the wife and cousin of Jan (Season 2)
- Verónica Moral as Leonor "Leo" Grandes Álvarez, Roque's controlling ex-wife and mother of his daughter Alba. She leaves for the United States with Alba, but returns with news that their daughter is ill. (Season 2)
- Álex Yuste as Márquez, former boyfriend of Fer and student of Zurbarán (Season 1 — Season 2)
- Carlos Wu as Mr. Taeming, Jan's Chinese father who owns a convenience store in town (Season 1 — Season 2)
- Santiago Meléndez as Mr. Cabano, Cesar Cabano's abusive father (Season 1 — Season 2)
- Aura Garrido as Erica, Alma's former love. (Season 3)
- Miriam Giovanelli as Lucía, Julio's former girlfriend and student of Zurbarán (Season 3)
- Ximena Suárez as Marta, gymn teacher at Colegio Zurbarán (Season 2 — Season 3)
- Carlos Velasco as Rodrigo "Rodri" Prieto, Julio's enemy and Lucía's brother (Season 2 — Season 3)
- María Casal as Marisa, Adolfo's ex-wife who he leaves for Loli and Roque's mother (Season 2 — Season 4)
- Mark Schardan as Thomas, Irene's boyfriend (Season 3 — Season 4)
- Aida de la Cruz as Andrea, a cancer patient (Season 4)
- Olivier Morellón as Oliver, Zurbarán student (Season 1 — Season 4)
- Itaca López Martínez as Laura, Zurbarán student (Season 1 — Season 4)
- Arantxa Aranguren as Matilde Martínez, Gorka's mother. She becomes the school janitor, much to the embarrassment of Gorka. (Season 1 — Season 5)
- Jaime Pujol as Alonso de la Torre, Julio and Reuben's father (Season 4 — Season 5)
- Marina Gatell as Sandra, stripper and mother of Martin's daughter (Season 5)
- Ramiro Blas as Ricardo López, Clara's boyfriend and Zurbarán's pumbler (Season 6)
- Diego Ramírez as Diego, Paula's love interest and librarian assistant (Season 6)
- Teresa Arbolí as Dolores "Loli" Prieto, Paula and Isaac's mother and Adolfo's former lover (Season 1 — Season 6)

Guest stars and cameos
- Nacho Cano as himself
- El Sueño de Morfeo are themselves
- Liz Solari and Tomás de las Heras as Charlotte and Gonzalo respectively, from the show *Champs 12*.
- Ana Fernandez and Luis Fernández are themselves; crossover with the television series *Los protegidos*.
- Despistaos as themselves
- DJ Nano as himself

Source (edited): "http://en.wikipedia.org/wiki/F%C3%ADsica_o_Qu%C3%ADmica"

Goenkale

Goenkale is a Spanish soap opera in Basque language, produced by Pausoka Entertainment and ETB, which is broadcast every Monday and Tuesday on Basque Radio-television's first channel, ETB 1. Set up in an imaginary Basque seaside town, the title of the serial is the name of the main street in that town. First broadcast in 1994, almost 3,000 episodes have been made so far, and it is one of the most successful programmes of ETB 1.

In the beginning every chapter lasted 30 minutes and they were broadcast from Monday to Friday. Then the Friday episode was removed. Since 2004 two one hour long episodes are broadcast every Monday and Tuesday. Then thirty minute episodes (half a normal episode) are repeated in the afternoon everyday.

Arralde

Arralde is the fictional seaside town where Goenkale is set up. The programme is recorded at Euskal Telebista's Miramon studios and other outside locations, mainly Orio and Tolosa. In addition, images of different Basque towns are shown, Mutriku, Lekeitio, Orio, Getaria and Bermeo. Next to Arralde, there is another imaginary town named Amaru, often mentioned by the characters of Goenkale.

The main street of the town is called Goenkale, and the scenes set on this main street are recorded at Euskal Telebista's studios, where there is an outdoor set. During the 16 seasons it has been on air, many different sets and scenarios have been used, including the Boga Boga tavern, Maitiena Hotel, Bar Sobia, a txoko (gastronomic society), a videoclub, a bakery, the police station, and the houses of different characters. Currently, they are recording the sixteenth season.

Goenkale. Origins

Goenkale kicked off in 1994, with a bad relationship between the Lasa brothers. Jose Mari, owner of hostel-restaurant Boga-Boga, and Martin, owner of a shop. After their mother dies, they find out that the will favours one of them, and that fact destroys the relationship between both families. The situation becomes unbearable until the sudden death of Martin, one of the two brothers.

XVI. Season. Synopsis

The relationship between the Madariaga brothers, German and Kandido, is getting worse as the time goes by. Even more when German finds out that his brother sent him to jail, as a revenge after German's behaviour made his live a nightmare. Kandido is not in the mood forgiveness, but Unai's death, German's youngest son, makes him think it over. Kandido becomes the manager of the family business, with the help of Abel their father. Meanwhile, they will make a big effort to get out of the drug dealing business. Things at home don't work better. After many years of lies and betrayals Alizia and Kandido's marriage is over. Alizia loves German, and she needs to live with him, now that everybody knows that German is the father of Naia, Alizia's youngest daughter. Their new life together isn't going to be an easy way. Not everybody is will accept this reality.

At the same time, Magistrate Klaudia Egaña, the new mayor of the town, gets to Arralde after Koldo's refuse in the city hall. She is going to do her best to boost the town, and all the inhabitants will support her. Only a woman is going to confront her. Leonor. She doesn't want to lose her lands for the new mayor's projects. Even that, Leonor will be defeated by Klaudia, a woman who doesn't like to lose at anything, cold and selfmade.

Moreover, nobody knows that Klaudia is back because of the dark Petralanda case. A case following an accident where many people were dead, and in which she worked as a magistrate. This case also brings back Olga, German's first wife, with a new name, with a new face. She is going to try to clarify the case, and the death in strange circumstances of her youngest son, linked for sure to the case.

Cameo Appearances and anecdotes

Goenkale has had such a big impact in the basque society, that some seasons ago, the Butchers Association asked to eliminate one of the plot referred to a case about adulterated meat. The issue even reached the parliament.

Another season, when a kid was kidnapped, the TV station received hundreds of calls warning that the boy had been seen in Gernika, (real town of the actor), and complaining about the incompetence of the Ertzaintza, (the Basque police), arguing that they were following false statements.

The actress playing the character of Maria Luisa was once rebuked in the street by her wickedness in the series. The actress received a letter from a man in which she was warned that some other characters wer lying to her. The man wrote this address in the envelope: Maria Luisa Galardi. Boga-Boga tavern. Arralde. Gipuzkoa. A smart postman that had the letter added in the envelope the address of the TV station, and that's how the letter got into the hands of the actress.

During its 16 seasons, many celebrities made special appearances in the series. Influential people in the Basque society such as the basque chefs Juan Mari Arzak, Martin Berasategi, Pedro Subijana and Hilario Arbelaitz. ETB stars like Andoni Aizpuru, Klaudio Landa, Yolanda Alzola, Ilaski Serrano, Julio Ibarra and Josu Loroño.

Singers as Mikel Urdangarin or Gari, the writer Pako Aristi, pelota player Mikel Goñi, football player Bittor Alkiza, rower Izortz Zabala, or the bertsolari Sebastian Lizaso also took part in different chapters.

The most popular cameo appearance without any doubt, was the one in 2004 where the presidents of the Real Sociedad and Athletic of Bilbao, football teams (Jose Luis Astiazaran and Fernando Lamikiz) made an intervention. It had a huge media attention, and Goenkale and both presidents appeared in the national papers as well as many Spanish TV news.

Among the last cameo appearances can be mentioned, TV clowns Txirri, Mirri and Txiribiton, climbing world champion Patxi Usobiaga, football player Iñigo Díaz de Cerio, former Miss Spain Natalia Zabala, alpinist Edurne Pasaban, bertsolari Andoni Egaña, best seller writer Karmele Jaio and the cast of the successful TV series Go!azen.

Well known actors in Goenkale

During its 16 seasons, lots of actors starred in Goenkale. Some of them are very well known not only in the Basque Country but also abroad. Actors as Barbara Goenaga, Aitor Luna, Miren Ibarguren, Jose Ramon Soroiz, Joseba Apaolaza, Veronica Moral, Ane Aseginolaza, Iñaki Beraetxe, Gorka Otxoa, Isidoro Fernandez, Iker Galartza or Carlos N'Guema.

Character biographies

Season 13 began in September 2006 and will end in mid July 2007. The main characters this season have been the following:

Other characters of the 13th season
- Ane Pikaza => *Arrate*
- Ander Etxebeste => *Jon / Ion*
- Manu Etxarri => *Asier*
- Aitor Aldabeltreku => *Edorta Garitonandia*
- Manu Uranga => *Aritz*
- Itziar Orrea => *Mertxe*
- Lierni Fresnedo => *Begoña*
- Asier Oruesagasti => *Kevin*
- Ziggy Dockerty => *Milena*
- Dorleta Urretabizkaia => *Ana Popesku (Milena's mother)*
- Na Gomez => *Pello*

Former characters
- José Ramón Argoitia => Gregorio
- Anabel Arraiza => Sara
- Loli Astoreka => Begoña
- Maite Bastos => Margarita
- Maiken Beitia => Mila
- Iñaki Beraetxe => Mikel
- José María Berasategi ==> Txapas
- Teresa Calo => Koro
- Mañu Elizondo => Agustín
- David Errasti => Don Luis
- Isidoro Fernández => Ibon
- Iker Galartza => Tomax
- Kepa Gallego => Nestor
- Aintzane Gamiz => Elene
- Mikel Garmendia => Jose Mari
- Bárbara Goenaga => Ainhoa
- Miren Gojenola => Amaia
- Arantxa Gurmendi => Hortentsi
- Jose Kruz Gurrutxaga => Karlos
- Gorka Igartua => Guti
- Iñake Irastorza => Teresa
- Anuska Lasa => Ane
- Mikel Laskurain => Felix 'Puskas'
- Niko Lizeaga => Gaizka
- María Luzarraga => Mertxe
- Irune Manzano => Pilar
- Judit Mariezkurrena => Olga
- Oihana Maritorena => Teresa
- Pedro Otaegi => Eusebio
- Manex Rekarte => Julen
- Pilar Rodríguez => Petra
- Martxelo Rubio => John Kepa
- José Ramón Soroiz => Martin
- Itziar Urretabizkaia => Lutxi (2003-)
- Paul Zubillaga => Xabier

Source (edited): "http://en.wikipedia.org/wiki/Goenkale"

Gominolas

Gominolas is a Spanish television series that follow the lifes of the members of *Gominolas* (a fictional children pop band, much like Parchís, in the '80s at the Spanish speaking countries) but as adults, 20 years later. It was aired on Cuatro from november to december 2007

Source (edited): "http://en.wikipedia.org/wiki/Gominolas"

La Hora Chanante

La Hora Chanante (*The Whamming Hour* or *The Amazing Hour*) is a Spanish comedy television show aired through the cable/satellite local version of the Paramount Comedy channel. Each episode is a half hour long and consists of a series of unrelated sketches (both acted out and animated) and a story featuring some celebrity which helps keep continuity throughout the program. Episodes used to be released on a monthly basis until 2006, when the show was discontinued. However, reruns are aired frequently through Paramount Comedy as well as Localia, and in December 2007, Paramount Comedy Spain and Universal Pictures launched a pack of two DVDs with the best moments of "La Hora Chanante" and some extras, an unreleased (episode 51), deleted scenes, stickers and a comic drawn by Joaquín Reyes.

It was created and directed by comedian from Albacete Joaquín Reyes, who also played the celebrities portrayed in each episode, thus serving as a show host. Many of the show's cutscenes were drawn by Lalo Kubala and Carlos Areces, both known for their work in the Spanish satire magazine El Jueves.

The staff responsible for La Hora Chanante started in September 2007 a new show with a similar format in the public channel La 2, called Muchachada Nui.

Sections

Each one of the programs consists of more or less stable sections (since only the really stable ones are **Testimonios**, **Retrospecter** and **Hever vs. Clever**), plus some varied sketches. The main ones would be (some with the original name in Spanish and the translation next to it):

- **Testimonios** (**Testimonies**): impressions of celebrities, usually old-fashioned (1980s and early 1990s), who monologues an autobiography in a humorous tone, and tends to speak using a thick manchego accent. Also, the character whose impression is made in the Testimonials section of the program is the presenter of the program the following month.
- **Retrospecter**: Made out of images taken from old black and white films and tv shows without license (an example would be Mr. Wong in Chinatown with Boris Karloff), which is dubbed with commentaries in the line of the program, taking advantage of the situations for the original plot. This is a stable section in the program, and honors the habitual character of Caesar Romero.
- **CÑÑ**: the character Eduardo Torrijos, interpreted by Joaquín Reyes, is a parody of a special broadcaster of an informative, informing about the news (most of it being gastronomic news) for channel "CÑÑ TV" parody of CNN TV, but

with the letter Ñ, mostly used in the Spanish language.
- **Cuéntaselo a Asun (Tell it to Asun)**: Velilla Valbuena incarnates Asun, a presenter of "vespertine" magazine in which various characters go an tell about their life stories, always with a comical vision; it also has an "historical" version with popular past people like Franz Kafka, Archduke Franz Ferdinand of Austria, Karl Marx and Friedrich Engels, amongst others.
- **Doctor Alce (Dr Moose)**: Two animation characters drawn by Joaquín Reyes (*Doctor Alce*/*Doctor Moose*) and **Señor Cabeza (Mr. Head)** a talking lump of jelly that lives with him) carry out conversations about TV themes, such as Batman series, starred by Adam West (in fact Doctor Alce considers himself an expert in these themes, but is not that expert at all).
- **Economía Chanante y el Payaso (Chanante Economy and the Clown)**: In his first stage **the Clown** with **Chanante Economy** gave financial advice, and then a variety of other themes (videoclips, the creation of his videogame, etc.), always carried out by *the Clown*, with a tacky sense of humor that characterizes him.
- **El Gañán** (the most accurate translation would be **Redneck**): Section similar to the one of **the Clown** (in fact it could be considered a spin-off of it) in which "el Gañán" explains, in its unique way, some subjects like immigration, hospitality, miracles, modern art, etc., and even gives lessons like a **Curso de Tollinas (Leasons of "Tollinas")** in which it teaches how to slap people in the neck in the correct way or **Cómo hablar en gañán (How to speak in gañán)**, his own way to speak Spanish.
- **Superñoño**: Animation series created by Joaquín Reyes in which a "superhero" who most of the time is "asobinado" (i.e. laying) in the bed explains his superpowers to us and his personal "adventures".
- **Hever versus Clever**: the bloopers of the program and the final section of it.
- **El Rincón de Agnes (The Agnes place)**: Joaquín Reyes interprets Agnes, that makes commentaries about fictional books, for example "El Hombre que meó Coca Cola" (The Man who pee Coke).
- **Bizcoché y Ojos de Huever**: Another animation created by Joaquín Reyes, with two kind of American rednecks that engage in an absurd conversation.
- **Minutos musicales (Musical Minutes)**: Animation created by Carlos Areces, it's a kind of humorous and bizarre music video clip.

List of episodes

- Episode 1 Starring: an old man (well, Joaquín Reyes as an old man)
- Episode 2 Starring: David Hasselhoff
- Episode 3 Starring: Nacho Duato
- Episode 4 Starring: Carl Lewis
- Episode 5 Starring: Mikhail Gorbachev
- Episode 6 Starring: Vanilla Ice
- Episode 7 Starring: Antonio Gala
- Episode 8 Starring: Michael Jackson
- Episode 9 Starring: Margareth Thatcher
- Episode 10 Starring: Francis Ford Coppola
- Episode 11 Starring: Mick Jagger
- Episode 12 Starring: Pat Morita
- Episode 13 Starring: John McEnroe
- Episode 14 Starring: Montserrat Caballé
- Episode 15 Starring: Ronald Reagan
- Episode 16 Starring: Axl Rose
- Episode 17 Starring: Anatoly Karpov
- Episode 18 Starring: Dolly Parton
- Episode 19 Starring: Salman Rushdie
- Episode 20 Starring: Liza Minnelli
- Episode 21 Starring: Mr T
- Episode 22 Starring: Fernando Jiménez del Oso
- Episode 23 Starring: Muammar al-Gaddafi
- Episode 24 Starring: Stephen King
- Special 25 programs
- Episode 26 Starring: Nadia Comăneci
- Episode 27 Starring: Björk
- Episode 28 Starring: Karl Lagerfeld
- Episode 29 Starring: Sara Montiel
- Episode 30 Starring: Bill Cosby
- Episode 31 Starring: Richard Clayderman
- Episode 32 Starring: Nana Mouskouri
- Episode 33 Starring: Vladimir Tkachenko
- Episode 34 Starring: Barbra Streisand
- Episode 35 Starring: Mike Tyson
- Episode 36 Starring: Tim Burton
- Episode 37 Starring: Mario Alberto Kempes
- Episode 38 Starring: Hugh Hefner
- Episode 39 Starring: Ágatha Ruiz de la Prada
- Episode 40 Starring: David Copperfield
- Episode 41 Starring: Bill Gates
- Episode 42 Starring: Sarah Ferguson
- Episode 43 Starring: Nikki Lauda
- Episode 44 Starring: José Luis Moreno
- Episode 45 Starring: Madonna
- Episode 46 Starring: Hugo Chavez
- Episode 47 Starring: María Jesús Grados
- Episode 48 Starring: Antonio Lopez
- Episode 49 Starring: Raffaella Carrà
- Special 50 Episodes Starring: Lorenzo Lamas
- Extra DVD La Hora Chanante Episode 51 Starring: Yoko Ono

Source (edited): "http://en.wikipedia.org/wiki/La_Hora_Chanante"

La que se avecina

La que se avecina is a Spanish television comedy that depicts the life of the inhabitants of *Mirador de Montepinar* (roughly translated as *Woodland Viewpoint*), a fictional apartment building in the outskirts of Madrid. Both its argument and cast is heavily based on Aquí no hay quien viva, as the former ended when Telecinco bought Miramón Mendi, the series production company.

Source (edited): "http://en.wikipedia.org/wiki/La_que_se_avecina"

Las noticias del guiñol

Las noticias del guiñol ("The news of guignol") was a satirical news programme that aired on Canal+ (since 1995) and Cuatro (since 2005) in Spain. It is somewhat based on a similar programme airing on its sister Canal+ network in France, *Les Guignols de l'info*, in that it features latex puppets. Latex casts may be shared among countries with local celebrities being used as anonymous citizens in foreign shows. It was initially hosted by the puppets of Marta Reyero and Hilario Pino, the real hosts of the channel daily news. Later, its host was a facsimile of Michael Robinson, an English-born football pundit; and in the final seasons it was conducted by the puppet of Iker Jiménez (a presenter of the channel).

While Penélope Cruz has made some appearances, the program generally focuses on prominent athletes and political figures. Among other figures, the program features Pau Gasol, Raúl, Luis Aragonés, Florentino Pérez, Joan Laporta, Fernando Alonso, José Luis Rodríguez Zapatero, Mariano Rajoy, María Teresa Fernández de la Vega, José Bono, Pasqual Maragall, and Josep-Lluís Carod-Rovira. International figures who regularly appear include David Beckham, Ronaldo, Ronaldinho, Samuel Eto'o, Louis Van Gaal (who instead of a head has a cube made of bricks, probably an allusion to his well-known stubbornness) George W. Bush, Condoleezza Rice, Tony Blair, Silvio Berlusconi and Pope Benedict XVI.

Historically, prominent characters have included Felipe González (occasionally appearing as Cantinflas), José María Aznar and Jordi Pujol.

One of the most often quoted phrases attributed to former prime minister José María Aznar - *"¡España va bien!"* (literally "Spain is doing well").

While most programmes on Canal+ were scrambled for non set-top box subscribers, *Las noticias del guiñol* was broadcast unscrambled.

In November 2005 Canal+ ceased to exist as a partially encrypted terrestrial television channel (although it continued to exist on the Digital+ satellite platform). It was replaced by Spain's fifth national terrestrial channel Cuatro, the newest member of Jesús de Polanco's Sogecable media empire. Although the *guiñoles* were one of the very few programmes to make the transition from Canal+ to Digital+, the programme was rebranded for the new channel as *Los guiñoles de Canal+*. The programme started being shown on the free-to-air channel Cuatro. Since 2006, they were included as a section in the late-night show "Noche Hache". Its production ceased at the same time as that show, in july 2008.

The programme has won "Premio Ondas", the most prestigious TV prize in Spain to the scriptwritters: Fidel Nogal and Gonzalo Tegel.

Source (edited): "http://en.wikipedia.org/wiki/Las_noticias_del_gui%C3%B1ol"

Los Serrano

Los Serrano is a Spanish television drama comedy which premiered on April 22, 2003 and is played on the channel Telecinco. It tells the story of the Serrano family, who lives in Round Santa Justa No 133, located in the fictional neighborhood of Santa Justa, in the Ribera del Manzanares, in Madrid. The success of the series in Spain and in several other countries in Europe and elsewhere helped launch the career of actor and musician Fran Perea, who acts in the series and sings its tune song, "1 más 1 son 7".

Plot

Diego Serrano, a widower and a single father of three sons, marries his first love Lucía Gómez who in turn has two daughters. The Gómez women move in with the Serranos, and the series follows the everyday lives of the new Serrano-Gómez family and their circle of friends in their homes, in the children's school and in their family-run tavern the 'Serrano Brothers'.

Main cast and characters

Serrano's Family

- Diego Serrano (Antonio Resines), the head of the family and a tavern entrepreneur.
- Marcos Serrano (Fran Perea), Diego's eldest son who falls in love with his stepsister Eva. He is living in France with Eva
- Guillermo Serrano (Víctor Elías), Diego's second eldest son.
- Curro Serrano (Jorge Jurado) , Diego's youngest son.
- Santiago Serrano (Jesús Bonilla), Diego's hot-headed older brother who runs the tavern with him.
- Lourdes "Lourditas" Salgado (Goizalde Núñez)
- Santiaguí , Santiago and Lourdes's son

Capdevila's Family

- Lucía Gómez (Belén Rueda), Diego's second wife, a school teacher.
- Eva Capdevila (Verónica Sánchez) , Lucía's eldest daughter. She is

currently living in France with Marcos.
- Teté Capdevila (Natalia Sánchez), Lucía's younger daughter.
- Carmen Casado (Julia Gutiérrez Caba), Lucía's mother.

Martínez's Family
- Fructuoso "Fiti" Martínez (Antonio Molero), Diego and Santiago's best friend, a car mechanic.
- Raúl Martínez (Alejo Sauras), Fiti and Candela's son and the best friend of Marcos.
- Asunción "Choni" Martínez (Pepa Aniorte) Fiti's sister
- José Luis Salgado (Javier Gutiérrez), Lourditas's brother and Choni's husband
- África Sanz (Alexandra Jiménez), on/off relationship with Raúl.

Blanco's Family
- Candela Blanco (Nuria González), Fiti's ex-wife and Lucía's colleague.
- Ana Blanco (Natalia Verbeke), Candela's younger sister.
- Andrés Blanco (Jorge Fernández Madinabeitia), Candela's brother.

Awards and nominations
- **Atv Awards**
  - 2004: Best Actor (Antonio Resines) - **WON**
  - 2004: Best Direction - **Nominated**
  - 2004: Best Fiction Program - **Nominated**
- **Fotogramas de Plata**
  - 2004: Best TV Actor (Antonio Resines) - **WON**
  - 2004: Best TV Actress (Belén Rueda) - **Nominated**
- **Ondas Awards**
  - 2004: Best Series - **WON**
- **Spanish Actors Union**
  - 2006: Television: Lead Performance, Female (Belén Rueda) - **Nominated**
  - 2006: Television: Performance in a Minor Role, Female (Alexandra Jiménez) - **Nominated**
  - 2005: Television: Lead Performance, Male (Antonio Resines) - **Nominated**
  - 2005: Television: Supporting Performance, Male (Antonio Molero) - **Nominated**
  - 2004: Television: Lead Performance, Male (Antonio Resines) - **Nominated**
  - 2004: Television: Performance in a Minor Role, Male (Manolo Caro) - **Nominated**
  - 2004: Television: Supporting Performance, Male (Jesús Bonilla) - **Nominated**
  - 2004: Television: Supporting Performance, Male (Antonio Molero) - **Nominated**
- **TP de Oro**
  - 2004: Best Actor (Antonio Resines) - **Nominated**
  - 2004: Best Actress (Belén Rueda) - **Nominated**
  - 2004: Best National Series - **Nominated**
- **Zapping Awards**
  - 2004: Best Actor (Antonio Resines) - **WON**
  - 2004: Best Actress (Belén Rueda) - **Nominated**

Source (edited): "http://en.wikipedia.org/wiki/Los_Serrano"

Los hombres de Paco

Los hombres de Paco' (English: *Paco's Men*) is a Spanish comedy television series, originally aired from 9 October 2005 to 19 May 2010 on the Antena 3. The series has also been broadcast in Argentina, Czech Republic, Poland, Hungary, Morocco, Romania, Serbia, Italy, Slovakia and Turkey. It was created by Daniel Écija and Álex Pina, and starred numerous actors, primarily Paco Tous and Pepón Nieto.

Season 6
Season 7
Season 8
Season 9

Cast and characters
- Paco Tous as **Francisco "Paco" Miranda** (2005–2010)
- Pepón Nieto as **Mariano Moreno** (2005–2010)
- Juan Diego as **Don Lorenzo Castro Riquelme** (2005–2010)
- Laura Sánchez as **María Jose "Pepa" Miranda Ramos** (2008–2010)
- Cristina Plazas as **Marina Salgado** (2008–2010)
- Federico Celada as **Curtis Naranjo** (2005–2010)
- Carlos Santos as **José Luis Povedilla Turriente** (2005–2010)
- Neus Sanz as **Margarita "Rita" Peláez** (2005–2010)
- Mario Casas as **Aitor Carrasco Menendez** (2007–2010)
- Goya Toledo as **Reyes Sánchez-Bilbao** (2010)
- Benjamín Vicuña as **Decker** (2010)
- Patricia Montero as **Lisa "Lis" Peñuelas Sánchez** (2010)
- Marcos Gracia as **Daniel Andradas** (2010)
- Ángela Cremonte as **Amaia Mondragon** (2010)
- Álex Hernández as **Gregorio "Goyo"** (2010)
- Asier Etxeandía as **Blackman** (2009–2010)
- Miguel de Lira as **Félix Montejo** (2008–2010)
- Adriana Ozores as **Dolores "Lola" Castro León** (2005–2009)
- Hugo Silva as **Lucas Fernández** (2005–2010)
- Michelle Jenner as **Sara Miranda Castro** (2005–2010)
- Clara Lago as **Carlota Fernández** (2007–2008)
- Marián Aguilera as **Silvia Castro León** (2005–2010)
- Neus Asensi as **Bernarda González** (2005–2007)
- Aitor Luna as **Gonzalo Montoya** (2005–2009)
- Enrique Martínez as **Enrique "Quique" Gallardo** (2005–2009)
- Jimmy Castro as **Nelson Amadú** (2009)

Source (edited): "http://en.wikipedia. org/wiki/Los_hombres_de_Paco"

Mis adorables vecinos

Mis adorables vecinos (Spanish for ``My Lovely Neighbors´´) is a Spanish Sitcom. It revolves around the life of a Spanish family and their two neighbors.

Characters
- Mariano: The father.
- Lolis: The mother, she works at a boutique owned by her and her best friend.
- Rafael (Rafa): The bigger son, during some episodes in the show he works as a car mechanic in his own garage.
- Sheila: Mariano and Lolis' middle child, a professional singer.
- Cuckys: Lolis´ best friend.
- Charlie: Rafa's best friend, a poor class guy with a hippie look.
- Poncho: Rafa's friend, who comes from a rich family.
- Ernesto: Mariano's neighbor, a wealthy plastic surgeon.

Source (edited): "http://en.wikipedia.org/wiki/Mis_adorables_vecinos"

Muchachada Nui

Muchachada Nui is a Spanish TV show, consisting of unrelated sketches that use absurd and surrealistic humor. It is broadcast on "La 2 de Televisión Española". It is the sequel of La hora Chanante, that first aired on Paramount Comedy (Spain).

Name

Since Paramount Comedy owned the rights of the previous program, including its name, "La Hora Chanante", a new name was needed.

In an interview , the actors explained that "Muchachada Nui" is a combination of "muchachada", a common word in their manchego vocabulary meaning "a group of lads", and "nui" from "ojete nui", as in "cuando te pica el ojete porque no te has lavado bien" (when your asshole itches because you haven't washed it well).

Actors

The same actors that appeared in "La Hora Chanante" appear in "Muchachada Nui". However, their characters are not the same, as a result of the copyright issue. The ones that appear most often are: Julián López, Ernesto Sevilla, Raúl Cimas, Carlos Areces, and the director and creator Joaquín Reyes.

Format and sections

As in "La Hora Chanante", each program is presented by a characterization of a famous star facing some kind of trouble. This story is divided in parts, and, between them, other sketches are shown. Some of these sections are repeated throughout the weeks, though only "Celebrities" and "Mundo viejuno" are always present. Many of these sections were present in "La Hora Chanante" with a different name.

Sections

Celebrities: Joaquin Reyes characterizes a famous person, and speaks about their life from a humorous point of view, always with a manchego accent. This character introduces the other sections throughout the program. It is the equivalent of the old "Testimonios" section in "La Hora Chanante".

Mundo viejuno (Elder world, viejuno being a word from their manchego vocabulary): Old movies - generally B movies, such as Mr Wong in Chinatown, with Boris Karloff - are redubbed with a plot that echoes the original one and at the same time takes advantage of the images to create a comic effect. It is the equivalent of the old "Retrospecter" in "La Hora Chanante".

Las aventuras del joven Rappel (The adventures of young Rappel): A parody of the show Smallville, where the main character is Rappel (a famous fortune-teller in Spain) who is in the process of discovering his powers. Rappel is played by Carlos Areces.

Al fresco (A play on words; "Al fresco" means "Outdoors", but "fresco" is also a term for a cheeky person): Marcial Ruiz Escribano (played by Ernesto Sevilla) is a "gañán" (which could be best translated as "redneck") that explains several topics related with rural life. It is the equivalent of "El Gañán" in "La Hora Chanante".

El bonico del to (Something like "The utterly beautiful"): El Bonico (played by Carlos Areces) is a characters that explains his view points about society. He is a hoity-toity yet conservative man worried about values and aesthetics in present society.

Tú eres el protagonista (You are the protagonist): A parody of a talk show, hosted by Pedro Bonilla (played by Julián Pérez).

El perro muchacho (The dog-boy): Perro Muchacho is a local superhero with a dog-face.

Riken Sproken: A tacky character that thinks about life situations that are soul-depressing.

Gaticos y Monetes (Little Cats and Little Monkeys, monete being a manchego word): The takeouts. It is the equivalent of the old "Hever vs Clever" section in "La Hora Chanante".

Cartoons

Enjuto Mojamuto: A nerd's life experiences and adventures, always concerning the Internet. Created by Joaquin Reyes.

La cinta VHS (The VHS tape): A VHS tape remembers the pre-DVD times. Created by Joaquin Reyes.

Los Klamstein (The Klamsteins):

The Klamsteins are a family consisting of Frederik Klamstein (the bread-winner), Amy Klamstein (a she-gorilla), Angela-Lansbury Klamstein (the daughter), and Junior Klamstein (the son).In an interview, Carlos Areces, the creator of this cartoon, stated that the gorilla was taken from the film Congo, and Angela-Lansbury Klamstein from the actress Angela Lansbury.

Loqui and the Loquer Loqui is a teenager groupie having constant mood changes, who talks to 'Man in the mirror' (the man in her bedroom's mirror).

Characters

El hombre asqueroso (The disgusting man): An apparently normal man, who dresses in an elegant and tidy way. However, he has a "disgusting" accent. Played by Julián López.

El espantajo de los melones(The scarecrow of the melons): Previously known as "El loco de las coles" (The cabbage-obsessed man).

El señor McGlor (Mr McGlor): Previously known as Señor Glor (Mr Glor). Played by Antonio Tato.

Internet

La Hora Chanante's videos used to be massively shared through pages such as YouTube, so Muchachada Nui, in an original strategy for a TV show, decided to upload almost all of their sketches to its YouTube channel.

The 24th October, 2007, they started their own web, were all their sketches can be found. There is also a blog, Enjuto Mojamuto's page in Twitter, forums and other things.

In November 2007, a Enjuto Mojamuto's space in Twitter was created. Since then, it has become the most-followed one in Spain, with 2400 followers, and the 31st in the world.

Source (edited): "http://en.wikipedia.org/wiki/Muchachada_Nui"

Plats bruts

Plats bruts (from catalan "*dirty plates*") was a comedy television series issued for TV3. The story talk about the life of Josep Lopes and David Güell. The show was co-produced by Kràmpack, El Terrat and Televisió de Catalunya.

Source (edited): "http://en.wikipedia.org/wiki/Plats_bruts"

Sé lo que hicisteis...

Sé lo que hicisteis... (**SLQH**), (In English, **I know what you did...**) is a daily afternoon comedy show aired by La Sexta. From late 2007 to mid 2009 it was the most viewed of this channel not counting sport broadcasts. The program originally dealt with Spanish sensationalist media ("Prensa del corazón") with humour and criticism, however the two hours program also deals with internet clips, politics and reports from social events. It airs from Mondays to Fridays at 3:25 PM, after laSexta|Deportes *(Sporting News)*.

Patricia Conde is the presenter of the show. Ángel Martín was the co-presenter until January 21 2011. Miki Nadal is a daily co-presenter who front his own section. Dani Mateo (Ángel's friend from Paramount Comedy) and Berta Collado are the new incorporations from November 2007. Dani Mateo comments on politics and sports; Berta Collado reports on important events. Pilar Rubio, the reporter, abandoned the program in 2010, and was replaced by Cristina Pedroche.

History

SLQH started broadcasting on March 30 of 2006, during the first week of broadcasts from La Sexta. Initially titled *"Sé lo que hicisteis la última semana"* and aired weekly on Wednesday night. It quickly became one of the most successful areas of the channel, both in praise and in ratings which has doubled the average audience of La Sexta. The show is recorded in studies of Globomedia, producer of the program, located North East of Madrid.

From April 9 2007 and as of 2011 the show is now broadcast daily at 3.25 PM to 5.10 PM. The program has undergone several changes, the most important has been critique of videos from other channels, its hallmark during these four years (to cover more content to focus on their own) to the point emit only a tiny number in the program.

Presenters and collaborators

Patricia Conde is the program's main presenter, appearing for the duration of the entire program. She is accompanied by different co-presenters, each one of which heads their own section. She takes on a dizzy-blonde-with-psychotic-traits type role; for example: she claims it's normal to talk to puppets, she leaves the table with few or no excuses (this is actually a humorous way to go to the commercial break), she often hits her co-workers because *"La Sexta's boss says that violence and sex raises audience figures, and I don't like you, so..."*. Patricia sometimes makes comments about how to kill people or how to hide a corpse.

Ángel Martín and Patricia Conde (presenters of the show).

- Berta Collado: After being one of the reporters of the show, Berta now has her own section called "Yo Te Promociono" ("I Promote You") in which she interviews celebrities that are specially interested in getting promotion from the show. She also imitates many Spanish TV

personalities. Berta also hosts the show when Patricia is away.
- Miki Nadal: in his section "Soy el que más sale en televisión del mundo" (I am the one who knows the most about TV in the world), Miki shows clips often extracted from the Internet or taken from foreign shows (usually American and Japanese). Whereas Ángel is polite and serious -most of the time; he will make an occasional suden and gross comment for humorous effect-, Miki is rude, loud and is politically incorrect to his female co-workers. He prefers physical and toilet humor and his catchphrase is "¡Hggg, Ay Omá, qué rica!" (*Snort* Oh ma, So tasty! *grunt*) when talking about beautiful girls.
- Dani Mateo: Ángel's friend, he comments on the news of the day with irony and humour called '¿Qué Está Pasando?', in a similar style to Angel's. Patricia calls him "enchufado" or "avioncitos" ("plugged in", which means a person who has obtained his/her job through the influence of another person as opposed to his / her own merit or qualifications: and "Little Planes", because his section is headed by an animation of paper planes).
- Cristina Pedroche: Another reporter of the program; she goes to events and interviews celebrities. Her technique of interviewing is composed of pretend naivety and innocence to approach characters who may have been lambasted in the previous section.
- Paula Prendes: The second reporter of the show; As well as Cristina, she attends any kind of events in which celebrities are involved. After summer 2010 she decided to leave the show and join a radio project in Europa FM. A week after she was back to SLQH.
- David Guapo
- Leo Harlem
- Jordi Mestre

Ex-collaborators

- Ángel Martín: Was the co-presenter of the show and his section was the most viewed. Ángel showed clips from other programs, (sensationalist programs) that he analyzed, commenting on frequent mistakes and sensationalist hoaxes with irony and sarcasm. Ángel was too serious for Patricia, and he was often annoyed by Patricia's behavior. He frequently repeats expressions, such as"¡Madre mía!" (My mother!) and "Te voy a decir una cosa" (I'm going to tell you something...) (placing a finger on his lips).
- Alberto Casado: He criticized their own show in the same manner as Ángel Martín (who Alberto pretends to dislike) did. He too left the show in January 2011.
- Pilar Rubio: She was the show's main reporter; she goes to events and interviews celebrities. Her technique of interviewing was composed of pretend naivety and innocence to approach characters who may have been lambasted in the previous section. She appears with [[Dance Hall Crashers]]'s, "Lost Again" and on her video header sounds "Big Mouth"; formerly her theme song was "Find My Baby" by Moby.
- Pepe Macías: Used to do parody shorts about celebrities' lives. Later in his section "Regreso al Pasado" (Back to the Past), a pun of the film *Back to the Future*, looked back at celebrity / gossip magazines and television from a specific year.

Controversies

The show has been controversial around the shows aired on Telecinco, Antena 3 and even Telemadrid or TVE.

The host of the sensationalist and controversial show *Aquí hay tomate*, Jorge Javier Vázquez claimed to have been a victim of hatred and discrimination for being homosexual. Vázquez accused *Sé lo que hicisteis...* of continuous defamations and accusations of alcoholism.

The show was accused of airing *pornography* at Midday, when actually the show aired a clip from Antena 3 *¿Dónde estás corazón?*, a late night *"rosa"* program where Dinio and Carmen de Mairena were shown in sexual attitude.

The program have received criticism in the Peruvian TV program *Amor, Amor, Amor* where some jokes about Tigresa del Oriente were labelled as discrimination. Peruvian singer Wendy Sulca was also mocked in the show but was invited to a Peruvian TV show to answer the mockery, in the show she presented a new music video together with child singers and "you-tube stars" Chacaloncito and Melanie la Burbujita where they asked to be let alone and for the why of the mockery of their culture while dancing in their traditional polleras that had been called "pieces of curtain" in *Sé lo que hicisteis...*

Source (edited): "http://en.wikipedia.org/wiki/S%C3%A9_lo_que_hicisteis.."

Vaya Semanita

Vaya Semanita is a Spanish weekly sketch comedy show that is broadcast by the second network of Euskal Telebista (ETB 2) since 2004.

Cast

First and second seasons
- Óskar Terol
- Nerea Garmendia
- Iñigo Agirre
- Alejandro Tejería
- Andoni Agirregomezkorta
- Gorka Otxoa
- Elisa Lledó
- Julian Azkarate
- Maribel Salas
- Santi Ugalde
- Kike Biguri

Seasons 3-5
- Andoni Agirregomezkorta
- Iker Galartza
- Javier Antón
- Itziar Lazkano
- Laura de la Calle
- Manuel Elizondo
- Diego Pérez
- Susana Soleto
- Antonio Salazar
- Raúl Poveda
- Julián Azkarate
- Carlos Urbina
- Ángela Moreno
- Elisa Lledó
- Ramón Merlo

Season 6
- Andoni Agirregomezkorta
- Iker Galartza
- Javier Antón
- Itziar Lazkano
- Manuel Elizondo
- Diego Pérez
- Susana Soleto
- Ramon Merlo
- Itziar Atienza
- Pablo Salaberria

Source (edited): "http://en.wikipedia.org/wiki/Vaya_Semanita"

¡Ay, Señor, Señor!

¡Ay, Señor, Señor! (Oh, Lord, Lord!) was a 26-episode Spanish television series transmitted by Antena 3 between 1994 and 1995. It tells of the adventures of a modern, open-minded priest, portrayed by the actor Andrés Pajares. The series kick-started several acting careers, including those of Javier Cámara and Neus Asensi.

The singer Massiel starred in four episodes and Paloma Cela in nine, with many other actors and actresses making regular or guest appearances.

Source (edited): "http://en.wikipedia.org/wiki/%C2%A1Ay,_Se%C3%B1or,_Se%C3%B1or!"

Enrique Jardiel Poncela

Enrique Jardiel Poncela (October 15, 1901, Madrid – February 18, 1952) was a Spanish playwright and novelist who wrote mostly humorous works.

In 1932-33 and 1934 he was called to Hollywood to help with the Spanish-language versions shot in parallel to the English-language films.

His daughter, Evangelina, wrote a book entitled, *Mi Padre* (My Father).

Writings
- *La Tournee de Dios*
- *Esperame en Siberia, Vida Mia!*
- *Pero ... ¿hubo alguna vez once mil virgenes?*
- *El Libro del Convaleciente*
- *Eloísa está debajo de un almendro*
- *Una Letra Protestada y dos Letras a la Vista*
- *Pirulis de la Habana*
- *Usted Tiene Ojos de Mujer Fatal*
- *DOS Farsas y una Opereta*
- *Exceso de Equipaje*
- *Cuatro corazones con Freno y Marcha Atrás*

Source (edited): "http://en.wikipedia.org/wiki/Enrique_Jardiel_Poncela"

Juan José Carbó

Juan José Carbó Gatignol (March 19, 1927 – May 15, 2010) was a Spanish cartoonist and one of the great masters of Spanish comics, who won the 2005 Universidad de Alicante "premio Notario del Humor" ("Notary of Humor Award"), and signed all his Illustrations with his pseudonym, **Carbó**. Carbó drew in the mediums of newspapers, journals, children's magazines and even an adult magazine called *Reseo* (*Cattle Magazine*).

Early life and education

Juan José Carbó Gatignol, known primarily by his autographed signature of Carbó on his artwork, was born in Sueca, Spain on March 19, 1927. From an early age, he expressed an interest in art and received tutelage from his art teacher Alfredo Carlos, who also was a painter.

In 1939 near the end of the Spanish Civil War, Carbó moved with his family to Valencia where his father died. Carbó took drawing classes at the Escuela de Bellas Artes de San Carlos (San Carlos School of Fine Arts). In 1944, Carbó obtained work as a security guard and continued taking free night classes.

Comic strip career

In 1949, Carbó began his career as a cartoonist with the protagonist, *Don Homobono*, who appeared in a magazine published by Cubilete Gong. Carbó also drew for a children's magazine supplement. After performing military service, he caught on with the *Editorial Valenciana* newspaper where Carbó created characters *Robustiano Fortachón* and the surrealistic *El Penado 113*. During the 1950s, he was one of this newspaper's more influential "Escuela Valenciana" (Valencian School) members. His illustrations were considered precise yet with a simple didactic method. While at the "Escuela Valenciana", Carbó influenced fellow contemporaries such as José Sanchis Sinisterra, Soriano Izquierdo, Enrique Cerdán and others.

Carbó started drawing cover arts and specialized in "¿Cuánto sabes?" ("How much do you know?"), "¡Ocurre cada cosa!" ("Everything occurs"), and sports biographies. His work was also displayed in a thumbnailed section of the *Editorial Bruguera* publishing house. His character, *Ivanchito*, appeared in the pocket-sized paperback cartoon *Jaimito*.

During the 1970s, Carbó drew *Plácido Guerra*. After getting weary of work at *Editorial Bruguera*, he left for *Diario de Valencia* daily where he continued drawing his *Placido Guerra* for its in-house supplement. Carbó also drew for the labor journal, *El Coet*, and adult magazine, *Reseo* (*Cattle Magazine*).

From 1993 to 1994, Carbó drew *Tonet* as a comic strip character in the Education Journal of the Spanish Consellería de Cultura (Ministry of Culture).

Later life and death

Throughout his life, Carbó stayed active with a Spanish group known as "Asociación de Autores de Cómic de España", AACE (literally Association of Authors of Comics in Spain). He worked the group into his daily schedule and regularly attended its meetings. Carbó also exhibited his illustrations at the "TebeoSpain" at the Biblioteca Nacional de San Miguel de los Reyes (National Library of St. Michael the Archangel) in Valencia.

Carbó remained a painter and continuously worked as a security clerk from age 17 to 65. He continued to hold his first art instructor, Carlos, with esteem into his latter years and was proud to be born on St. Joseph's day.

Carbó died at the age of 83 on May 15, 2010.

Source (edited): "http://en.wikipedia.org/wiki/Juan_Jos%C3%A9_Carb%C3%B3"

Pedro Antonio de Alarcón

Pedro Antonio de Alarcón y Ariza (1833-1891) was a nineteenth century Spanish novelist, author of the novel *El Sombrero de Tres Picos* ('The Three-Cornered Hat', 1874). The story is an adaptation of a popular tradition and provides a lively picture of village life in Alarcón's native region of Andalusia. Alarcón wrote another popular short novel, *El capitán Veneno* ('Captain Poison', 1881). He produced four other full-length novels. One of these novels, *El escándalo* ('The Scandal', 1875), became noted for its keen psychological insights. Alarcón also wrote three travel books and many short stories and essays.

Alarcón was born in Guadix, near Granada. In 1859, he served in a Spanish military operation in Morocco. He gained his first literary recognition with *A Witness' Diary of the African War (1859-1860)*, a patriotic account of the campaign.

Works

- Cuentos amatorios.
- El final de Norma: novela (1855).
- Descubrimiento y paso del cabo de Buena Esperanza (1857).
- Diario de un testigo de la Guerra de África (1859).
- De Madrid a Nápoles (1860).
- Dos ángeles caídos y otros escritos olvidados.
- El amigo de la muerte: cuento fantástico (1852).
- El año en Spitzberg.
- El capitán Veneno: novela.
- El clavo.
- El coro de Angeles (1858).
- La Alpujarra (1873)
- El sombrero de tres picos: novela corta (1874).
- El escándalo (1875).
- El extranjero.
- El niño de la Bola (1880).
- Historietas nacionales.
- Juicios literarios y artísticos.
- La Alpujarra: sesenta leguas a caballo precedidas de seis en diligencia.
- La Comendadora.
- La mujer alta: cuento de miedo.
- La pródiga
- Lo que se oye desde una silla del Prado.
- Los ojos negros.
- Los seis velos.
- Moros y cristianos.
- Narraciones inverosímiles.
- Obras literarias de Pedro Antonio de Alarcón. Volumen 2
- Obras literarias de Pedro Antonio de Alarcón. Volumen 1
- Obras literarias de Pedro Antonio de Alarcón. Volumen 3
- Poesías serias y humorísticas
- Soy, tengo y quiero.
- Viajes por España.
- Últimos escritos.

Source (edited): "http://en.wikipedia.org/wiki/Pedro_Antonio_de_Alarc%C3%B3n"